Bibliographic information published by the German National Library:

The German National Library lists this publication in the National Bibliography; detailed bibliographic data are available on the Internet at http://dnb.dnb.de .

Imprint:

Copyright © 2018 GRIN Verlag
Print and binding: Books on Demand GmbH, Norderstedt Germany
ISBN: 9783668807143

This book at GRIN:

https://www.grin.com/document/442590

Palaniappan Sellappan

Learn C++ Programming. Through Examples

GRIN Verlag

GRIN - Your knowledge has value

Since its foundation in 1998, GRIN has specialized in publishing academic texts by students, college teachers and other academics as e-book and printed book. The website www.grin.com is an ideal platform for presenting term papers, final papers, scientific essays, dissertations and specialist books.

Visit us on the internet:

http://www.grin.com/

http://www.facebook.com/grincom

http://www.twitter.com/grin_com

LEARN C++

Through Examples

PROF. DR. P. SELLAPPAN

MALAYSIA UNIVERSITY
of Science and Technology

Preface

The C language was originally designed to support procedure-oriented programming. It was subsequently extended to C++ to support object-oriented programming (OOP). The symbol ++ in C++ indicates that it is an extension of C. C++ supports all features of C, as well added capability to support OOP. Thus you can C++ for both procedure-oriented and object-oriented paradigms.

C++ is one of the most popular programming languages available today. With it, you can develop all sorts of applications such as scientific and business applications and games. It is also a popular language for mircroprogramming and interfacing with hand-held devices and electronic circuit boards and for developing IoT applications.

This book is based on Microsoft Visual C++ 2017 but will equally apply to other versions of C++.

This text is intended for beginners and intermediate users. It starts from the basics, but progresses rapidly to the more advanced features. So whether you are a beginner or an experienced C++ programmer, this book will help you master the essentials of C++ programming very quickly. The text is written in an easy-to-read style and contains numerous examples to illustrate the programming concepts. It also contains exercises for practice at the end of each chapter.

Acknowledgements

I would like to gratefully acknowledge the contributions of several people who have in one or another assisted me in the preparation of this book. I would like to thank all my IT students and colleagues for their valuable input and feedback in the preparation of this manuscript.

My grateful thanks also go to Professor Dr. Premkumar Rajagopal, President of the Malaysia University of Science and Technology for giving me the opportunity, freedom, encouragement and support that I needed in the preparation of this manuscript. I would like to especially thank him for creating and nurturing an environment that actively promotes learning, research, teamwork and personal development. His dynamic leadership is greatly appreciated.

Last but first I would like to thank God for giving me the desire, motivation, interest, passion, strength and guidance to successfully complete this manuscript.

Dr. P. Sellappan
Professor of Information Technology
Dean of School of Science and Engineering
Provost of Malaysia University of Science and Technology

About the Author

Dr. P. Sellappan is currently Professor of Information Technology, Dean of School of Science and Engineering, and Provost of the Malaysia University of Science and Technology. Prior to joining Malaysia University of Science and Technology, he held a similar academic position in the Faculty of Computer Science and Information Technology, University of Malaya, Malaysia.

He holds a Bachelor in Economics degree with a Statistics major from the University of Malaya, a Master in Computer Science from the University of London (UK), and a PhD in Interdisciplinary Information Science from the University of Pittsburgh (USA).

Working in the academia for more than 30 years, he has taught a wide range of courses both at undergraduate and postgraduate levels: Principles of Programming, Advanced Programming, Programming Languages, Data Structures and Algorithms, System Analysis and Design, Software Engineering, Human Computer Interaction, Database Systems, Data Mining, Health Informatics, Web Applications, E-Commerce, Operating Systems, Management Information Systems, Research Methods, Mathematics and Statistics.

Professor Sellappan is an active researcher. He has received several national research grants from the Ministry of Science and Technology and Innovation under E-Science and FRGS to undertake IT-related research projects. Arising from these projects, he has published numerous research papers in reputable international journals and conference proceedings. Besides, he has also authored over a dozen college- and university-level IT text books.

As a thesis supervisor, he has supervised more than 70 Master and PhD theses. He also serves in editorial/review boards of several international journals and conferences. He is also chief editor of the Journal of Advanced Applied Sciences and the Plain Truth magazine. He is a certified trainer, external examiner, moderator and program assessor for IT programs for several local and international universities.

Together with other international experts, he has also served as an IT Consultant for several local and international agencies such as the Asian Development Bank, the United Nations Development Program, the World Bank, and the Government of Malaysia. His professional affiliation includes membership in the Chartered Engineering Council (UK), the British Computer Society (UK), the Institute of Statisticians (UK), and the Malaysian National Computer Confederation (MNCC).

Contents

Chapter 1

Introducing C++

Learning Outcomes:

After completing this chapter, the student will be able to

- *Explain the programming model.*
- *Describe the Visual C++ Integrated Development Environment.*
- *Edit, Compile and Run C++ programs.*
- *Describe the different parts of a C++ program.*

1.1 About Visual C++ 2017

Developed by Microsoft, Visual C++ 2017 is one of the most powerful and popular general-purpose programming languages available today. With C++, you can develop all sorts of applications – be it scientific, business or games.

Visual C++ is an extension of the C programming language originally developed by Brian Kernighan and Dennis Ritchie at the Bell Telephone Laboratories in the 1970s. Whereas C was designed to support procedure-oriented programming, C++ supports both procedure-oriented and object-oriented programming (OOP) paradigms. Thus C++ has the advantages of both programming paradigms.

This book is based on Visual C++ 2017, but it will equally apply to other versions of C++.

1.2 Programming Model

Computer programs typically read **input** data from input devices like the keyboard, **store** and **process** the data, and send **output** (results) to output devices like the monitor. This **input-processing-output-storage** (**IPOS**) is called the programming model (see Figure 1.1).

A computer program consists of a set of **statements (commands, instructions)**. We will use these terms interchangeably in this text. Some of these commands perform the computations while others perform input/output. The program can be simple or complex depending on the tasks that it needs to perform to solve a problem.

A typical C++ program consists of **include directives, define directives, variable declaration, assignment, control flow,** as well as **input/output statements**. We will give a sample C++ program to explain these statements at the end of this chapter.

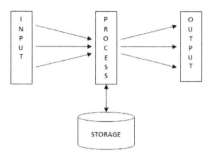

Figure 1.1: Input-Processing-Storage-Output

1.3 Editing, Compiling & Running Programs

A computer program goes through several stages - editing, compiling, linking and running – before it generates useful output.

First, you type (edit) the program, then compile it, then link it with other programs (e.g., typically library functions), and then run it. Figure 1.2 shows the steps involved, the tools used, and the output at each step.

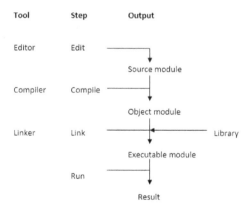

Figure 1.2: Editing, Compiling and Running Programs

To simplify programming, Visual C++ 2017 provides a user-friendly **Integrated Development Environment (IDE)** for editing, compiling, running and debugging programs. The IDE provides several user-friendly menus to help users manage these (and other) tasks. This greatly simplifies the programming task.

You can edit, compile and run a program using the following steps:

1) Type your program using the Editor and save it. The program you created is called the **source program** (or **source code**).

2) Compile the program. The compiler will compile the source program to an **object program** (or **object code**). The compiler will also generate other useful information the **linker** needs to link the object code with the library functions the program needs. The linked program is called an **executable**. It is in the final form - ready to run. You can breeze through all these steps simply by clicking the ▶ Local Windows Debugger icon located at the top (just below the Menu strip).

1.4 Starting Visual C++

The steps for editing, compiling and running a Visual C++ program are as follows:

Select Start > Programs > Visual Studio 2017

You will see the screen

Click on Visual Studio 2017.

You will see the **Start Page**

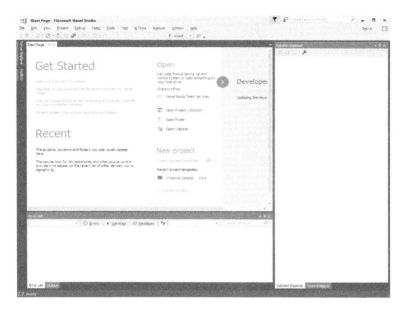

Click on **Create new project** (highlighted in blue) and this will take you to a **New Project** Window shown below.

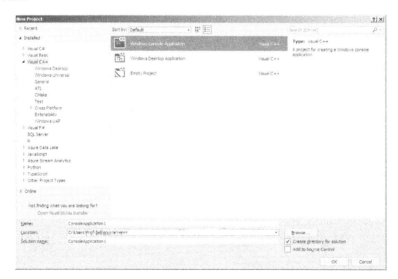

Select Visual C++ >> Windows Console Application.

4

At the bottom, you will see Name, Location and Solution name.

You can use the default file name **ConsoleApplication1** or supply another name.

Then click **OK**.

You will see the **Integrated Development Environment (IDE)**

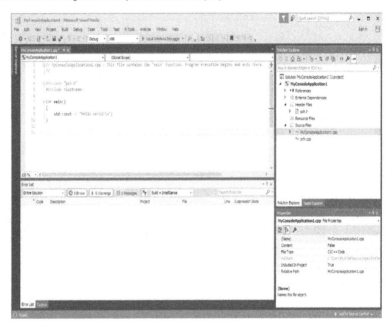

The IDE shows several things:

Located at the top are several **Menu** items (**F**ile, **E**dit, etc.). You can use the Shortcut keys (such as **F** for File, **E** for Edit) to launch these programs.

Each Menu item comes with a **drop-down** menu. The drop down menus for File, View, Build and Debug are shown below (there are others besides these).

Just below the Menu ribbon are several icons for Opening New Project, Saving and Running a program.

Below these two Menu ribbons are four windows:

The **Code** window on the left is where you type your code.

The **Error List** window below the Code window gives you information when your program compiles.

The **Solutions Explorer** window on the right shows the files related to your application (e.g. ConsoleApplication1).

6

The **Properties** window shows the properties for a selected item in the Solution Explorer.

1.5 Sample Programs

Program 1.1 gives you a flavor how a C++ program looks like. The line numbers on the left are for purposes of explanation only – they are not part of the code. The output is shown below the program.

Program 1.1

```
1    // This is a comment
2    // and so is this
3
4    // include directives
5    #include "pch.h"   // precompiled header file; it is required and must come first
6    #include <iostream>  // used for input/output
7    #include <string>    // used for string operations
8
9    // std is the standard namespace; used for grouping variables
10   using namespace std;
11
12   // main function; program execution starts here
13   void main()  // void means main will not return any value to the calling program
14   {  // begin code block
15       string name;   // declare a string variable
16       int age;        // declare an integer variable
17       cout << "Enter name: ";  // send prompt to monitor
18       cin >> name;             // read name from keyboard
19       cout << "Enter age: ";
20       cin >> age;
21       cout << name << ", you are " << age << " years old." << endl;  // send output to monitor
22   }  // end code block
```

Sample output:

```
Enter name: Sally
Enter age: 27
Sally, you are 27 years old.
```

Let's briefly explain the different parts of the program.

Comments begin with //. Comments are inserted into a program to make it readable. Comments can be *inline* or *whole line* comments. Whole line comments start on separate lines (e.g. line 1, 2 and 4); inline comments begin after a statement (e.g. line 13 to 18).

Directives begin with a sharp sign (#) and the keyword include (**#include**) followed by a header file (lines 5 to 7). Directives tell the C++ compiler to include certain **precompiled** header files needed to run the program. One of these header files is **pch.h** (line 5). This file is required to run all C++ programs and must be placed **before** all the other header files. (Earlier versions may use the standard application framework extensions **stdafx.h**).

Besides include directives, your program may also need #define directives for defining constants. For example #define n 7 means assign the value 7 to the variable n.

Namespaces are used for grouping variables to avoid clashes, especially in long programs. Most programs will need the **standard** namespace using namespace std; (line 10).

The **main function** begins with the a keyword such as `void main ()` (line 13). Program execution will always start at `main ()`. The prefix `void` tells that `main ()` will not return any value to the calling program, in this case the operating system (OS). You may also specify the return type `int` (in this case your type `int main ())`.

Code blocks are enclosed between a pair of braces (`{ }`) (lines 14 and 22). It contains a block of statements - as many statements as you need including none.

Declaration statements begin with keywords like `char`, `int`, `double`, `string`, etc. (lines 15 and 16). These statements specify the data types of the variables used in the program. All variables must be declared before they can be used.

Input statements begin with `cin >>` (lines 18 and 20) Input statements read data from the console (keyboard) and store them in variables. For example, `cin >> name` will read a name from the keyboard and store it in the variable `name`.

Output statements begin with `cout <<` (lines 17 and 19). Output statements send output to the console (screen/monitor). For example, `cout << name` will out the value stored in variable `name` to the monitor.

Note the direction of the input (>>) and output (<<) operators.

Return statements (if any) begins with the keyword **return**. It terminates a function and returns a value to the calling function. If the return type is `void`, the `return` statement can be dropped altogether as in the above program.

Program 1.2 produces the same output as Program 1.1, but here `main ()` function returns an integer value (0) to the calling program (OS). The return data type in Program 1.1 was `void` whereas the return type in Program 1.2 is `int`. You can choose to return nothing (`void`) as in Program 1.1 or choose to return an integer as in Program 1.2.

Program 1.2

```
// main() function returns an integer to the OS
#include "pch.h"
#include <iostream>
#include <string>
using namespace std;

// int tells main() will return an integer to the calling program (OS)
int main()
{
    string name;
    int age;
    cout << "Enter name: ";
    cin >> name;
    cout << "Enter age: ";
    cin >> age;
    cout << name << ", you are " << age << " years old." << endl;
    return 0;   // returns 0 (int) to the OS
}
```

The above programs are intended to give you a flavor how C++ programs look like. Don't worry, if you don't fully grasp the program code. We will explain these and others statements more fully in subsequent chapters.

Exercise

1. Explain the programming model using a simple scenario such as processing exam results, payroll, or withdrawal from an ATM machine.

2. Familiarize with the Visual C++ IDE: main menu, pull-down menus, short-cut keys, etc.

3. Explain the different part of a C++ program.

4. Write a "Hello world" program and run it.

Chapter 2

C++ Basics

Learning Outcomes:

After completing this chapter, the student will be able to

- *Explain the structure of a C++ program.*
- *Explain the different data types.*
- *Declare identifiers, variables and constants.*
- *Use operators and form expressions.*
- *Write assignment statements.*
- *Write input/output statements.*
- *Write and run simple C++ programs.*

2.1 Structure of C++ Programs

A typical C++ program takes the form:

```
#include <header file>        // include directive
...
#define variable expression   // define directive
...
using namespace std;          // declare namespace std

void main()                   // main function; returns no value
{  // starts code block
   // variable declarations

   // statements

}  //ends code block
```

The above structure shows three parts: #include directives, #define directives, using namespace std, and the main() function with code block enclosed by a pair of braces {}.

We will use Program 2.1 (in screenshot) to explain the various parts a C++ program. The line numbers on to the left are meant for purposes of explanation only – they are not part of the code. The output is shown below the program.

Program 2.1

```
1    // calculares area of a circle
2    // given the radius
3
4    // directives
5    #include "pch.h"      // this precompiled header file is required
6    #include <iostream>  // needed for input/output
7    #define pi 3.1412     // pi is assigned a constant value
8
9    using namespace std;  // this standard namespace is required
10
11   // main function; program execution starts here
12   void main()  // void type means main does not return any value
13   {  // code block starts here
14       double radius, area;                // declare variable of type double
15       cout << "Enter radius: ";           // send prompt to monitor
16       cin >> radius;                      // read radius from the keyboard
17       area = pi * radius * radius;        // calculate area
18       cout << "Area = " << area << endl;  // send output to minitor
19   }  // code block ends here
```

Here is a sample run:

```
Enter radius: 7.2
Area = 162.84
```

Let's briefly explain the different parts of the program.

Comments

Comments are inserted into a program to make it readable. Comments can be placed anywhere in a program. They begin with the compound symbol //. Comments can be *inline* or *whole line*. Inline comments appear after a statement (e.g. lines 5, 6 and 7). Whole line comments appear on separate lines (e.g. lines 1, 2 and 4). You can create a multiline comment by starting each line with //. Alternatively, you can use the pair /* and */ to span a comment on several lines.

Blank lines

Blank lines can be inserted anywhere in a program to separate code blocks and make the program readable (e.g. lines 3, 8 and 10).

Include directives

The #include directive tells the C++ compiler to include the specified *header files* (containing precompiled code). Directives start with a sharp sign # (e.g. lines 5-7). This program uses two header files - pch.h, and <iostream>. The header file pch.h which stands for **precompiled** header file is required to run C++ programs (earlier versions may use stdafx.h) . This file must be placed *before* the other directives. The <iostream> which stands for **input-output stream** is used for reading input from the console (keyboard) using cin >> and for writing output to the console (monitor) using cout <<.

The #define directive (line 7) tells the compiler to assign the constant value 3.1412 to the variable pi.

Functions

All C++ programs must have the `main()` function (line 12). Besides `main()`, a program may also define other functions (we will cover this in later chapter). The parentheses `()` following the function name are required even if the function has no parameters. The keyword `void` prefixed before `main()` function tells that it will not return any value to the calling program.

All statements (lines 13-18) in a function must be enclosed between a pair of curly braces `{ }`. A code block can contain any number of statements including none.

Namespaces

Namespaces are used for grouping variables and to avoid confusion when the same variable names are used in different namespaces. A namespace begins with the keyword `using`. The `using namespace std;` (line 9) uses the **standard** namespace required to run all C++ programs.

Declaration statements

All variables must be declared before they can be used in a program. Variables have data types such as `integer, float, double, char, string,` and `bool`. The data type tells how many bytes of memory a variable needs to store a value. The declaration statement `double area, radius;` declares `radius` and `area` as of type `double` (line 14).

Input/Output Statements

Input statements read input data from the console (keyboard). Output statements send output (results) to the console (monitor). The input statement `cin >> radius;` (line 16) reads an input value for `radius`. Similarly, the output statement in line 18 sends output to the monitor. Input statements begin with `cin >>`. Output statements begin with `cout <<`. Note the direction of the input >> and output << operators.

Assignment statements

Assignment statements take the form `variable = expression;`. The expression on the right-hand side of the assignment operator (=) is evaluated first, and the result is assigned to the variable (`area`) on the left-hand side. The statement in line 17 calculates and stores the result in the variable `area`.

Header files

Header files contain *precompiled* code to perform various tasks such as: math calculations, string processing, input/output. You will need one or more of these header files to compile and execute your program correctly. You only include those header files your program needs.

There are two types of header files: one using the file extension `.h` and the other without the extension. The header files with file extension `.h` are from the C language whereas those without the file extension are from the C++ language. C++ allows you to use both header files. Newer C++ header files starts with character 'c' as in `<cstdio>`.

2.2 Keywords, Identifiers & Variables

The C++ character set includes all keyboard characters: uppercase letters A to Z, lowercase letters a to z, digits 0 to 9, and other special characters such as #, %, &, >, * and the blank (or whitespace) character).

Identifiers are used to name constants, variables, function names, labels and classes. Identifiers are formed by combining letters (upper and lower case letters), digits, and the underscore (_). Identifiers must start with a letter or an underscore. Identifiers in C++ are **case-sensitive**. That means upper and lowercase characters are treated differently. So the variables name, Name, NAME are all different variables.

Variables are identifiers used to reference memory locations for storing and retrieving data items. The values stored in these locations can change during the course of program execution. Variables have data types such as char, string, int, double and bool. Different data types require amounts of memory. For example an integer variable requires 4 bytes of memory whereas a double variable requires 8 bytes of memory.

Keywords, also called **reserved words**, are identifiers which have predefined meanings. As such, they must only be used for their intended purpose. The list below gives the C++ keywords.

List of C++ keywords

asm	auto	break	case	char
class	const	continue	default	delete
do	double	else	enum	extern
far	float	for	friend	goto
huge	if	inline	int	interrupt
long	near	new	operator	private
protected	public	register	return	short
sizeof	static	struct	switch	this
typedef	union	unsigned	virtual	void
volatile	while			

2.3 Data Types

Variables must specify their data types. C++ supports several data types. The data type tells how many bytes of memory a variable needs to store data. The list below shows the data types and the range of values they can store.

C++ data types

Type Name	Bytes	Other Names	Range of Values
int	4	signed	−2,147,483,648 to 2,147,483,647
unsigned int	4	unsigned	0 to 4,294,967,295
__int8	1	char	−128 to 127
unsigned __int8	1	unsigned char	0 to 255
__int16	2	short, short int, signed short int	−32,768 to 32,767
unsigned __int16	2	unsigned short, unsigned short int	0 to 65,535
__int32	4	signed, signed int, int	−2,147,483,648 to 2,147,483,647
unsigned __int32	4	unsigned, unsigned int	0 to 4,294,967,295
__int64	8	long long, signed long long	−9,223,372,036,854,775,808 to 9,223,372,036,854,775,807
unsigned __int64	8	unsigned long long	0 to 18,446,744,073,709,551,615
bool	1	none	false or true
char	1	none	−128 to 127

signed char	1	none	−128 to 127
unsigned char	1	none	0 to 255
short	2	short int, signed short int	−32,768 to 32,767
unsigned short	2	unsigned short int	0 to 65,535
long	4	long int, signed long int	−2,147,483,648 to 2,147,483,647
unsigned long	4	unsigned long int	0 to 4,294,967,295
long long	8	none (but equivalent to __int64)	−9,223,372,036,854,775,808 to 9,223,372,036,854,775,807
unsigned long long	8	none (but equivalent to unsigned __int64)	0 to 18,446,744,073,709,551,615
enum	varies	none	See Remarks later in this article
float	4	none	3.4E +/- 38 (7 digits)
double	8	none	1.7E +/- 308 (15 digits)
long double	same as double	none	Same as double
wchar_t	2	__wchar_t	0 to 65,535

2.4 Constants

Constants are fixed literals; their values don't change during the course of program execution. C++ has four types of constants, namely, integer constants, character constants, floating-point constants and string constants. Below are some examples of each type.

Constant Type	Examples
Integer Constants Short integer Integer Unsigned integer Long integer	−99 −35 0 45 127 −999 −1 0 555 32767 1 256 11000 59874 203 12 3345 8989898 1
Character Constants	'$' '*' ' ' 'd' 'H' '1'
String Constants	"Name: " "Telephone No: "
Floating-point Constants	0.008 0.254E8 4.25E2

Constants are declared using the keyword `const` as follows:

```
const double PI = 3.14159; // const is a keyword
const string = "XYZ Solutions Provider";
const char esc = "\n";
```

2.5 Declaring Variables

All variables must be declared prior to their use in a program. Their declaration takes the form

```
data_type variable_list;
```

Here are some examples of valid variable declaration.

14

```
int a, b, c;            // declares 3 variables all of type integer
double amount, rate;
float f, g;
bool status;
char ch;
string name;
```

Variables of the *same type* can be declared on the same statement, but they must be separated by a comma.
The semicolon (;) at the end terminates the statement.

2.6 Initializing Variables

You can initialize variables when you declare them. Here are some examples of variable declaration and
initialization.

```
int m, n = 10;   // n is initialized to 10
double rate, total=0.0; // total is initialized to 0.0
float y = 123.45, z;
char response = 'n';
char color[6]= "green";
string s = "good day!";
bool flag = false;
```

The first statement declares m and n as integer variable but only n is initialized. The third statement declares
response as a character variable with the initial value n. The fourth statement declares color as an array
of characters with the initial value green. The last statement declares s as a string variable with the
initial value good day!

2.7 Operators

C++ has several built-in operators. Operators trigger a computation when applied to operands in an
expression. These operators include arithmetic, relational, logical and assignment operators.

Arithmetic Operators

Arithmetic operators are used with arithmetic calculations. The list below shows the arithmetic operators.

Arithmetic Operators

Operator	Meaning
−	Subtraction (also unary minus)
+	Addition
*	Multiplication
/	Division
%	Modulus (remainder operator)
--	Decrement
++	Increment

You can assign a positive or negative number to a variable by using a unary as shown below:

15

```
x = -10; // Assigns -10 to x
y = +30; // Assigns 30 to y, + sign normally not needed
```

Unary operators such as ++ and -- operate on a single operand. For example:

```
x++;    // same as x = x +1
y--;    // same as y = y - 1
```

Arithmetic operators have the following precedence:

Highest

++ --
- (unary)
* / %
+ -

Lowest

Relational Operators

The relational operators are as follows:

Relational operators

Operator	Meaning
<	Less than
<=	Less than or equal to
>	Greater than
>=	Greater than or equal to
==	Equal
!=	Not equal

A relational operation yields the value true or false. For example, if a = 8 and b = 3, the expression a < b will yield the value 0 and the expression a != b will yield the value 1.

Logical Operators

The logical operators are && (AND), || (OR) and ! (NOT).

Operator	Meaning
&&	Logical AND
||	Logical OR
!	Logical NOT

The table below summarizes the results of logical operations for Boolean variables x and y.

x	y	x || y	x && y
true	true	true	true
true	false	true	false
false	true	true	false
false	false	false	false

A logical operation in C++ will always result in 1 (true) or 0 (false).

Here are some examples of logical expressions for x = 1 and y = 0.

16

```
x || y      will yield 1
x && y      will yield 0
!x          will yield 0
```

You can combine arithmetic, relational and logical operators in an expression. For example, given a = 2, b = 3, c = 4 and d = 5, you can write as follows:

```
a < b || c < d     will yield 1
a > b && c > d     will yield 0
```

Assignment Operators

The assignment operator = is used in an assignment statement. Assignment statements take the form

```
variable = expression;
```

The expression on the right hand side of = is evaluated first and the result is assigned to the variable on the left hand side. The expression can be a constant, a variable or an expression.

Here are some examples of assignment statements:

```
age = 20;
salary = 1122.50;
amount = item_price * quantity;
```

Assignment operators can take compound forms such as *= and +=. If these operators are used, the variable on the left-hand side also acts as the first operand in the expression on the right-hand side. For example, if x = 8 and y = 5, you will have the following results.

Operator	Example	Equivalent to	Result
*=	x *= y	x = x * y	x will have the value 40
/=	x /= y	x = x / y	x will have the value 1.6
+=	x += y	x = x + y	x will have the value 13
-=	x -= y	x = x - y	x will have the value 3
%=	x %= y	x = x % y	x will have the value 3

Operator Hierarchy

The operator precedence from the highest to the lowest is as follows:

Operator Precedence

Operator Category	Operator
Unary	- -- ++
Arithmetic multiply, divide, remainder	* / %
Arithmetic add and subtract	+ -
Relational operators	< <= > >=
Equality operators	== !=
Logical AND	&&
Logical OR	||

2.8 Escape Sequences

An **escape sequence** character begins with a backslash (\) followed by a special character. Each escape sequence is treated as a *single* character. They are typically used with input/output statements. For example, to print a new line you can use the character \n ; and to beep a sound you can use the character \a. The list of escape sequences is as follows:

Escape sequences

Code	Meaning	Code	Meaning
\a	Audible bell	\v	Vertical tab
\b	Backspace	\\	Backslash
\f	Form feed	\'	Single quote
\n	New line	\"	Double quote
\r	Carriage return	\0	Null ASCII 0
\t	Horizontal tab		

2.9 Expressions

Expressions are formed by combining operators, variables and constants. We have already seen several examples of arithmetic and logical expressions. The expressions can be simple or complex. You can use parentheses to force the order of evaluation. An expression may contain spaces for readability. Here are some examples of valid expressions.

```
gross_pay - deductions
(basic_pay + hours * rate) - (socso + premium + loan)
(b * b - 4 * a * c) > 0
(sex == 'male' || sex == 'female') && age >= 21
```

Mixed-mode Expressions and Type Casting

When different data types are mixed in an expression, C++ converts the expression to the "longest" data type (i.e. one that requires most number of bytes).

Type casting can be used to force an expression to a specific data type. Type casting takes the general forms

```
(type) expression
type (expression)
```

Here are two examples:

```
amount = (float) quantity * price;
amount = float (quantity) * price;
```

2.10 Assignment Statements

Assignment statements take the form

```
variable = expression;
```

18

The expression can be simple or complex - a literal constant, a variable or some complex expression. I

Here are some examples.

```
pi = 3.1412;
amount = price & quantity;
interest = 0.07 & principle;
ans = 5.5 * ((a * b + c) - (x/y));
net_pay = (basic + hours * rate) - deductions;
weather = "It is bright and sunny today."
status = true;
bexp = (x < y) || (a > b);
```

2.11 Input/Output Statements

Input statements read data from the keyboard while Output statements write output to the monitor.

The header file used for performing input/output is <iostream>. This lets you read input data using cin >> and write output using cout <<.

cin and cout

Here are some examples.

```
// read input to a variable
cin >> variable;

// read input to 3 variables
cin >> variable1 >> variable2 >> variable3

// send output from a variable
cout << variable;

// send output from 3 variables
cout << item1 << item2 << item3
```

Here are more examples:

```
int a, b;
cin >> a;
cin >> a >> b;   // read 2 values and store them in a and b
cout << a;
cout << "Value of a is "<< a; // write message and value of a
cout << "\nValues of a and b are " << a << " " << b;
```

cin.get () and cin.put ()

You can also use the functions cin.get () and cin.put () to read or print single characters. They take the form:

```
cin.get();
cout.put();
```

Here are some examples:

```
char ch;              // declare character variable ch
cin.get(ch);          // read a character and store it in ch
ch = cin.get();       // another way to do
cout.put(ch);         // output the character in stored in ch
cout.put('y');        // output character 'y'
```

cin.getline()

You can also use the function `cin.getline()` to read a line of characters. They take the form:

```
getline(cin, line); // reads a line and stores in variable line
```

Here is an example.

```
string line;
getline(cin, line);   // read a line of characters
cout << line;         // print the line
```

setw(), setprecision() and fixed

You can format your output with `setw(n)`, `setprecision(n)` and `fixed` functions. To use these functions, you must include the `<iomanip>` header file. The `setw(n)` function prints output in n columns. The `setprecision(n)` prints numbers with a precision of n digits. The `fixed` function prints output with a fixed width.

endl;

The `endl;` statement terminates the line. It is equivalent to the escape sequence `\n` . Here are some examples.

```
cout << setw(7) << 12345;  // set column width to 7
```

The above statement will print 12345 with two blanks in front.

```
cout << "Name" << setw(10) << "Address";
```

The above statement will print Name and Address in 10 columns as follows:

```
Name        Address
```

The following statements illustrate the `setprecision(n)` function.

```
double amount = 123.4567;
cout << setprecision(2) << amount << endl;
cout << setprecision(5) << amount << endl;
cout << setprecision(7) << amount << endl;
```

The output is as follows:

```
1.2e+02   // same as 1.2 * 10²
123.46
123.4567
```

2.12 Sample Programs

Program 2.1 reads a (one word) name and age and displays the same.

Program 2.1
```cpp
// read name and age
#include "pch.h"
#include <iostream>
#include <string>
using namespace std;

void main()
{
    string name;
    int age;
    cout << "Enter name: ";
    cin >> name;        // will only read 1 word name
    cout << "Enter age: ";
    cin >> age;
    cout <<"\n" << name << ", your age is " << age << endl;
}
```

Sample output
```
Enter name: Sally
Enter age: 27

Sally, your age is 27
```

Program 2.2 reads a (multiple word) name and salary and displays the same. To read a string with multiple words such as a sentence, you need to use the statement `getline(cin, name);`. Using `cin >> name;` will only read the *first* word.

Program 2.2
```cpp
#include "pch.h"
#include <iostream>
#include <string>

using namespace std;

void main()
{
    string name;
    double salary;
    cout << "Enter employee name: ";
    getline(cin, name);  // reads a line of characters
    cout << "Enter employee salary: ";
    cin >> salary;
    cout << "\nName: " << name << endl;
    cout << "Salary $" << salary << endl;
}
```

Sample output

```
Enter employee name: Sally Nelson
Enter employee salary: 2570.90

Name: Sally Nelson
Salary $2570.9
```

Program 2.3 illustrates reading and printing characters and strings. Note the character handling functions get(ch) and put(ch) for reading and writing characters. The cin.ignore() function ignores (skips) the rest of characters in the input buffer.

Program 2.3

```cpp
#include "pch.h"
#include <iostream>
#include <string>
using namespace std;

void main()
{
    char ch;
    string word, line;
    cout << "Type a character: ";
    cin.get(ch);
    cout << "Character read is: " << ch << endl;
    cout << "\nType another character: ";
    cin >> ch;
    cout << "Character read is: ";
    cout.put(ch);
    cout << "\n\nConstant literal: ";
    cout.put('y');
    cout << endl;
    cout << "\nType a word: ";
    cin >> word;  // will only read the first word
    cout << "Word read is: " << word << endl;
    cin.ignore();  // this clears the buffer
    cout << "\nType a line: ";
    getline(cin, line);
    cout << "\nLine read is: " << line << endl;
}
```

Output

```
Type a character: w
Character read is: w

Type another character: q
Character read is: q

Constant literal: y

Type a word: nice
Word read is: nice

Type a line: nice day today

Line read is: nice day today
```

Program 2.4 illustrates several input/output functions: setw(), setprecision() and fixed. These functions are useful for formatting output. To use these functions, you need to include the #include <iomanip> directive.

Program 2.4

```
// illustrates formatting output using <iomanip> header file
#include "pch.h"
#include <iostream>
#include <string>
#include <iomanip>        // header for setting width and precision
using namespace std;

void main()
{
    string name = "Sally Nelson";
    int x = 12345;
    double y = 123.45678;
    cout << "Name: " << setw(12) << name << endl;
    cout << "Name: " << setw(17) << name << endl;
    cout << "x = : " << setw(7) << x << endl;
    cout << "x = : " << setw(10) << x << endl;
    cout << setprecision(6) << "y = " << y << endl;
    cout << setprecision(8) << "y = " << y << endl;
    cout << fixed;
    cout << name <<"\t" << x << "\t" << y << endl;
}
```

Output

```
Name: Sally Nelson
Name:        Sally Nelson
x = :   12345
x = :        12345
y = 123.457
y = 123.45678
Sally Nelson     12345    123.45678000
```

Program 2.5 illustrates arithmetic expressions and assignment statements. It also illustrates compound operators such as ++ and += and +* and the modulus (remainder) % operator.

Program 2.5

```
// illustrates compound operators ++ -- += etc.
#include "pch.h"
#include <iostream>
#include <string>
#include <iomanip>
using namespace std;

void main()
{
    int x = 123, y = 789, n = 5;
    double ans, p = 123.45, q = 987.67;
    ans = ((x + y) / n) + (n * (p + q));
    cout << setprecision(5) << "Answer = " << ans << endl;
    ans = x / y - p / q;
    cout << setprecision(7) << "Answer = " << ans << endl;
    ++x;  // increment x by 1
    --y;  // decrement y by 1
    cout << "x = " << x << "\t\ty = " << y << endl;
    x += y;  // same as x = x + y
    y *= x;  // same as y = y * x
    cout << "x = " << x << "\t\ty = " << y << endl;
    int hr = 17;
    cout << "hr % 12 = " << hr % 12 << endl;  // modulus operator %
}
```

23

Output

```
Answer = 5737.6
Answer = -0.1249911
x = 124          y = 788
x = 912          y = 718656
hr % 12 = 5
```

Exercise

1. Write a program to display the values of the following variables:

   ```
   int x = 5;
   float = 27.50;
   double = 579.78157;
   char color = 'y';
   string city = "Pittsburgh";
   ```

2. Write a program to read input data for the variables in Question (1) from the keyboard and display the same.

3. Write a program to read input data for the variables in Question (1) from the keyboard and display the same using the functions setw(), setprecision() and fixed.

4. Given x = 55, y = 75, z = 12, n = 2, write assignment statements to evaluate and display the following:

   ```
   (x + y) / n
   n * (x + (y / z))
   (7 * x + (y - z) - 2 * n)
   (x % 2) + (y % 7)
   ```

5. Trace the output for the skeleton code below.

   ```
   int z, x = 5, y = 7, n = 2;
   z = x + y;
   cout << "z = " << z << endl;
   x++;
   --y;
   cout << "z = " << x + y << endl;
   z = n * (x % y);
   cout << "z = " << z << endl;
   ```

24

Chapter 3

Pointers

Learning Outcomes:

After completing this chapter, the student will be able to

- *Explain pointers.*
- *Explain the pointer and address of operators * and &.*
- *Declare pointer variables.*
- *Perform pointer operations.*
- *Use pointers to pointers.*

3.1 Computer Memory

The computer memory has millions of bytes, each of which has an address. It is difficult to know or remember all these addresses because they are too many, but you're the computer operating system knows them all.

A **pointer** is a special variable that stores the *address* of a memory location (instead of data). That is, it points to a value stored at that location. For example, if the memory at location 5000 stores the memory *address* 5004, you can access the number (777) stored in that location using a pointer as shown in the figure below.

Pointer to data stored in memory location 5004

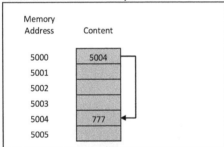

3.2 Declaring Pointers

Pointers, like ordinary/normal variables, must be declared before they can be used in a program. The general form for declaring a pointer variable is

```
data_type *ptr;
```

The data_type is any valid C++ data type such as char, int or double, and ptr is the pointer variable name. An asterisk (*) must precede a pointer variable. The asterisk indicates that ptr is pointer variable, not an ordinary variable.

The code below illustrates how pointers are declared:

```
// An asterisk precedes a pointer variable
char *cptr, ch; // cptr is a pointer variable; ch is a normal variable
int *iptr, i;
double *dptr1, *dptr2, d;
```

The first statement declares cptr as a pointer to a variable of type char and ch as a normal variable of type char. The second statement declares iptr as a pointer to an int variable and i as a normal variable of type int. The third statement declares dptr1 and dptr2 as pointers to a double variable and d as a normal variable of type double.

3.3 Pointer Operations

C++ uses two pointer operators: * and &. The **address of** operator & (a unary operator) returns the memory address of its operand while the **pointer** operator * (also a unary operator) returns the value stored in that address. Program 3.1 illustrates these pointer operations.

The statement

```
int *m, x = 567;
```

declares m as a pointer to an integer and x as a normal variable with the value 567.

The statement

```
m = &x;
```

stores the *address of* variable x which stores the number 567.

The statement

```
cout << "\nValue at x = " << *m;
```

prints the value stored in the variable pointed to by m. The expression *m accesses the value stored in variable x. That is, *m references the value stored in memory location pointed to by m. This way of referencing is called **dereferencing**.

Program 3.1

```
// pointer operations
#include "pch.h"
#include <iostream>
using namespace std;

void main()
{
    int *m, x = 567;
    m = &x;        // m stores the address of x
    cout << "\nValue of x = " << *m << endl;
}
```

Output

```
Value of x = 567
```

Pointer Expressions

Expressions involving pointers conform to the same rules as other C++ expressions. However, only addition and subtraction operations are permitted in a pointer expression.

We will now look at some pointer assignments, pointer arithmetic and pointer comparisons.

Pointer Assignments

A pointer variable, like any normal variable, can appear on the right hand side of an assignment statement. It can assign a value to another pointer variable of the *same type*.

Program 3.2 illustrates these ideas.

Program 3.2

```
// illustrates pointers
#include "pch.h"
#include <iostream>

using namespace std;

void main()
{
    int num = 5, *pointer1, *pointer2; // declares two pointers
    pointer1 = &num; // assigns address of num to pointer1
    pointer2 = pointer1; // assigns pointer1 to pointer2
    // displays num twice since pointer1 and pointer2 point to num
    cout << *pointer1 << "\t" << *pointer2 << endl;
}
```

Output

```
5      5
```

In the above program, both pointer1 and pointer2 store the same address (num). Therefore, the output for both *pointer1 and *pointer2 are 5. Note that in cout, we have prefixed the asterisk to both pointer1 and pointer2. Had we dropped the *, the program would display the *memory addresses* of the variables, not the *value* stored in num.

Pointer Arithmetic

Only two arithmetic operations – addition and subtraction – are allowed on pointers. To explain what occurs in a pointer arithmetic, let's declare a variable to hold the age of a person:

```
int age = 25;
```

This statement declares age as an integer variable with value 25. Let's suppose that the program has stored this number at memory address 1000 and we have a pointer ptr_age that points to age. Then, the statement

```
ptr_age++;
```

will increment the contents of `ptr_age` by 4 (as integer numbers takes 4 bytes). That means, `ptr_age` will now have the value 1004. As the integer value takes 4 bytes, C++ adds 4 to the pointer. So each time the pointer is incremented, it will point to the next integer. Similarly, when a pointer is decremented, it will point to the previous integer.

You can add an integer to or subtract an integer from a pointer variable. For example, if `pointer1` points to an integer array, then the statement

```
pointer1 = pointer1 + 7;
```

will cause `pointer1` to point to the seventh (from the current) element in the array.

Pointer Comparisons

C++ allows you to compare pointers of same type (i.e., pointers that point to the *same* data type, but not pointers of different data types. To illustrate, let's look at the code below.

```
int iptr1, iptr2, i1 = 5, i2 = 55;
double dptr1, dptr2, d1 = 7.0, d2 = 77;
iptr1 = &i1;
iptr2 = &i2;
dptr1 = &d1;
dptr1 = &d2;
```

Here, the comparison (`iptr1==iptr2`) is valid as since `iptr1` and `iptr2` are both of the same data type while the comparison (`iptr1==dptr2`) is invalid comparison as `iptr1` and `dptr2` are not of the same data type.

3.4 Pointers to Pointers

A pointer to a variable is called **single indirection**. If the pointer points to another pointer, we call it **double indirection**. The figure below illustrates single and double indirection.

Single indirection (pointer to normal variable)

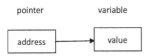

Double indirection (pointer to a pointer to a normal variable)

Here, the second pointer is a pointer to another pointer which points to a normal variable (containing a value).

In order to access the target value pointed to by a pointer to a pointer, the asterisk (*) operator is applied twice as follows:

```
int **twoptr;
```

This declaration tells the compiler that twoptr is a pointer to another pointer of type int.

Program 3.3 illustrates double indirection. It outputs the value 7 which is stored in variable num.

Program 3.3

```
// using single and double indirection
#include "pch.h"
#include <iostream>
using namespace std;

void main()
{
    int value, *firstptr, **secondptr;
    value = 7;
    firstptr = &value;          // firstptr points to a value
    secondptr = &firstptr;      // secondptr points to firstptr
    // display the value 7
    cout << *firstptr << "\t" << **secondptr << endl;
}
```

Output

7   7

3.5 Sample Programs

Program 3.4 shows how pointers can be used to refer to different areas of memory. The program declares two variables (var1 and var2) of type double and a pointer (ptr) to a double variable. The pointer is first assigned the address of var1. The first output statement displays the value stored in that address. Next the pointer is assigned the address of var2. The second output statement then displays the value stored in that address.

Program 3.4

```
// change value of pointer variable
#include "pch.h"
#include <iostream>

using namespace std;

void main()
{
    double var1, var2;
    var1 = 58.98;
    var2 = 60.02;
    double *ptr;
    ptr = &var1;
    cout << "The first number is " << *ptr << endl;
    ptr = &var2;        // makes ptr to point to var2
    cout << "The second number is " << *ptr << endl;
}
```

Output

```
The first number is: 58.98
The second number is: 60.02
```

Program 3.5 illustrates single and double indirection.

Program 3.5

```
// using single and double indirection
#include "pch.h"
#include <iostream>
using namespace std;

// int before main() tells main() will return an integer to the calling
// program (OS)
void main()
{
    int x = 55;
    int * ptr1, **ptr2;
    ptr1 = &x;
    ptr2 = &ptr1;
    cout << "ptr1: " << ptr1 << endl;  // print address of memory
    cout << "ptr2: " << ptr2 << endl;
    cout << "ptr1: " << *ptr1 << endl;
    cout << "ptr2: " << **ptr2 << endl;
}
```

Output

```
ptr1: 0046FDAC    // this is address in hexadecimal notation
ptr2: 0046FDA0
ptr1: 55
ptr2: 55
```

Program 3.6 displays a string using a pointer pt r.

Program 3.6

```
// display string using pointer
#include "pch.h"
#include <iostream>
#include <string>
using namespace std;

void main()
{
    string *ptr, s = "maritime";
    ptr = &s;           // tptr point to a value
    cout << *ptr << "\t" << endl;       // display the value 7
}
```

Output

```
maritime
```

Program 3.7 adds and multiplies two numbers using pointers.

Program 3.7

```
// add and multiply using pointers
#include "pch.h"
#include <iostream>
```

30

```cpp
#include <string>
using namespace std;

void main()
{
    int x = 7, y = 12;
    int *ptr1, * ptr2;
    ptr1 = &x;
    ptr2 = &y;
    cout << *ptr1 + *ptr2 << "\t" << *ptr1 * *ptr2 << endl;
}
```

Output

19   84

Program 3.8 access arrays using pointers. (Arrays are discussed in a later chapter.)

Program 3.8
```cpp
// access elements of array using pointer
#include "pch.h"
#include <iostream>
#include <string>
using namespace std;

void main()
{
    int *iptr, x[] = { 11, 22, 33, 44, 55 }; // x[] is an array
    string *sptr, s[] = { "violet", "indigo", "blue", "green",
                          "yellow", "red", "orange" };
    iptr = x;
    sptr = s;
    for (int i = 0; i < 5; i++)
    {
        cout << *iptr << "\t";
        iptr = iptr + 1;
    }
    cout << endl;
    for (int i = 0; i < 7; i++)
    {
        cout << *sptr << "\t";
        sptr = sptr + 1;
    }
    cout << endl;
}
```

Output

11	22	33	44	55		
violet	indigo	blue	green	yellow	red	orange

While C++ pointers offer tremendous power and flexibility to programmers, they need to be careful how they use them. If not used properly, pointers can result in code that is difficult to debug.

Exercise

1. Explain the following declarations:

```
int *a, *b, c;
double *f;
char *d, e;
int *x, **y;
```

2. Given x = 55, y = 77. Use pointers to compute the sum of x and y.

3. Trace the output for the code below.

(a)
```
int x, y, *z;
x = 5;
z = &x;
y = *z + 9;
cout << y;
```

(b)
```
double d1, d2 = 25.0, *d3, *d4;
*d3 = &d2;
*z = &x;
cout << *d3 + 7.2;
d1 = 20.0;
*d4 = &d1;
cout << *d3 + *d6;
cout << *d3 + *d4;
```

(c)
```
int x = 5, y = 7, z;
int *p1, *p2;
p1 = &x;
p2 = &y;
z = *p1 + *p2;
cout << *p1 << "\t" << *p2 << endl;
cout << "Sum = " << z << endl;
```

(d)
```
double d1 = 5.5, d2 = 7.7, *pd1, *pd2;
string s1 = "nice", s2 = "day", *ps1, *ps2;
pd1 = &d1;
pd2 = &d2;
ps1 = &s1;
ps2 = &s2;
cout << "Sum of d1 + d2 = " << *pd1 + *pd2 << endl;
cout << "Concat of s1 and s2: " << *ps1 << " " << *ps2 << endl;
```

Chapter 4

Control Flows

Learning Outcomes:

After completing this chapter, the student will be able to

- *Explain program control flow structures.*
- *Write programs using **if** and **switch** statements.*
- *Write programs using **for**, **while** and **do** loops.*
- *Choose which loop to use and when.*
- *Use nested loops.*
- *Use **break**, **continue** and **return** statements.*

Control flow (or structure) refers to the order of execution of statements in a computer program. Invariably all computer programs would require some decision making and looping. C++ has several **control structures** to make this possible. These include **sequence**, **decision making (selection)**, **looping (iteration/repetition)** and **jumps**.

4.1 Sequence Structure

The **sequence structure** is the simplest of these structures. In this structure, instructions are executed sequentially, starting from the first statement and ending with the last statement as in the code below.

```
rate = 5.0;                                     (S1)
hours = 25;                                      (S2)
pay = (double) hours * rate;                     (S3)
cout << "\nPay = $ " << pay << "\n";             (S4)
```

In this code, statement S1 is executed first, then statements S2, and so on. The structure has *one entry point* and *one exit point* as shown in Figure 4.1.

Figure 4.1: The sequence structure

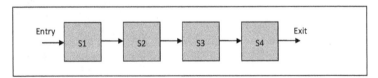

4.2 Decision Making

The **decision making (or selection) structure** allows statements to be executed non-sequentially. It compares two expressions, and based on the comparison, it takes different course of action. C++ provides several decision structures: `if`, `if-else`, `if-else if-else` and `switch`.

- **if**

The `if` structure has the general form

```
if (expression)
    statement;
```

The above statement can also be written more compactly as

```
if (expression) statement;   // spacing can be flexible
```

In this structure, **exp**ression is evaluated. If it evaluates to `true` (any *non-zero* value), `statement` is executed, and the `if` statement terminates. If the expression evaluates to zero (or `false`), control passes to the statement following the `if` statement. This structure also has one entry point and one exit point as shown in Figure 4.2.

Note that `statement` can take the form of a block containing several statements enclosed between a pair of braces `{ }`. The braces are required if there are two or more statements.

Figure 4.2: The `if` structure

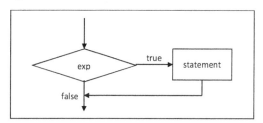

Example

```
if (hours > 40)
    hours = 40 + 2*(hours-40);
```

In this statement, if `hours` is greater than 40, its value is set to 40 plus twice the number `(hours-40)`. If `hours` is less than or equal to 40, control passes to the statement following the semicolon.

Example

```
if (job_code == '1')
{
    car_allowance = 200.00;
    housing_allowance = 800.00;
}
```

Here, the block of statements enclosed between the braces `{ }` will be executed only if `job_code` is equal to 1. Otherwise, control will pass to the statement following the statement block.

34

- ## `if-else`

The `if-else` structure has the general form

```
if (expression)
    statement_1;
else
    statement_2;
```

This statement can also be written more compactly as

```
if (expression)statement_1; else statement_2;
```

In this structure, **expression** is evaluated. If it evaluates to `true` (or non-zero), `statement_1` is executed, otherwise (i.e., `false` or zero) `statement_2` is executed. Note that the execution of the statements is mutually exclusive, meaning, only `statement_1` or `statement_2` is executed, but not both (as shown in Figure 4.3).

Figure 4.3: The `if-else` structure

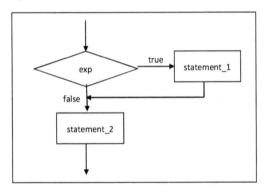

Example

```
if (sex == 'M')
    title = "Mr.";
else
    title = "Ms.";
```

The above code can also be written more compactly using the *immediate if* operator **?** as follows:

```
title = (sex == male) ? "Mr." : "Ms.";
```

Example

```
if (job_code == '1')
    rate = 5.00;
else
    rate = 7.00;
```

35

Here, if `job_code` is equal to 1 then `rate` is assigned the value 5.00; otherwise, `rate` is assigned the value 7.00.

Note that there is a semicolon (`;`) before the keyword `else`.

Example

```
if (job_code == '1')
{
    car_allowance = 200.00;
    housing_allowance = 800.00;
}
else
{
    car_allowance = 100.00;
    housing_allowance = 400.00;
}
```

- ## if-else if-else

The `if-else if-else` structure is a compound structure. It takes the general form:

```
if (expression_1)
    statement_1;
else if (expression_2)
    statement_2;
else if (expression_n)
    statement_n;
else
    statement;
```

Note: The key word `else if` is two words.

Here, **exp**ression_1 is evaluated. If it evaluates to `true`, `statement_1` is executed and the entire `if` statement is terminated. If `expression_1` evaluates to `false`, control passes to `else if` and `expression_2` is evaluated. If it is `true`, `statement_2` is executed and the rest of the `if` statement is terminated, and so on. Finally, if `expression_n` evaluates to `true`, `statement_n` is executed, otherwise `last_statement` will be executed. Again, only one of the statements in the block is executed.

Example

```
if (mark < 40)
    grade = 'F';
else if (mark < 50)
    grade = 'E';
else if (mark < 60)
    grade = 'D';
else if (mark < 70)
    grade = 'C';
else if (mark < 80)
    grade = 'B';
else
    grade = 'A';
```

36

Here, if mark is less than 40, grade is assigned the value F; if it is greater than or equal to 40 (but less than 50), grade is assigned the value E. The test continues for grades D, C, and B. Finally, if mark is equal to or more than 80, grade is assigned the value A.

Program 4.1 illustrates this structure.

Program 4.1

```
// program to test whether a transaction is a
// deposit, withdrawal, transfer or invalid
#include "pch.h"
#include <iostream.h>
using namespace std;

void main()
{
    double amount;
    char transaction;
    cout << "\nEnter transaction type(D, W, T): ";
    cin >> transaction;

    if (transaction == 'D')
    {
        cout << "\nDeposit:";
        cout << "\nEnter amount: ";
        cin >> amount;
    }
    else if (transaction == 'W')
    {
        cout << "\nWithdrawal:";
        cout << "\nEnter amount: ";
        cin >> amount;
    }
    else if (transaction-code == 'T')
    {
        cout << "\nTransfer transaction";
        cout << "\nEnter amount: ";
        cin >> amount;
    }
    else
    {
        cout << "\nInvalid transaction!";
        cout << "\nPlease enter the correct transaction code";
    }
}
```

Sample run:

```
Enter transaction type (D, W, T):   T

Transfer:
Enter amount: 555
Amount = 555
```

Program 4.2 is a shorter version of the above program.

Program 4.2

```
// Same as above but shorter
#include "pch.h"
#include <iostream>

using namespace std;
```

```
void main()
{
    double amount;
    char trans;
    cout << "Enter transaction type (D, W, T): ";
    cin >> trans;
    trans = toupper(trans);   // convert to uppercase
    if (trans == 'D')
        cout << "\nDeposit:\n";
    else if (trans == 'W')
        cout << "\nWithdrawal:\n";
    else if (trans == 'T')
        cout << "\nTransfer:\n";
    else
        cout << "\nInvalid transaction!\n";
    if (trans == 'D' || trans == 'W' || trans == 'T')
    {
        cout << "Enter amount: ";
        cin >> amount;
        cout << "Amount = " << amount << endl;
    }
}
```

- **switch**

The switch structure is a more elegant alternative to the compound if-else if-else structure. The switch structure lets you choose one (or more) of several alternatives. For this reason the switch statement is sometimes called *multiple-choice statement*.

The switch structure has the general form:

```
switch (expression)
{
    case exp_1:     statement_1;
                    break;          // break is usually required
    case exp_2:     statement_2;
                    break;
    default:        statement_n;
                    break;      // break in default may be omitted
}
```

where expression evaluates to an *integer,* a *character or a string constant.* Each alternative (except the default alternative) in the switch block is usually (but not always) terminated with a break statement. Figure 4.4 below illustrates this structure.

Each of the alternatives (except the default alternative) must have a case *label.* The default alternative (which is optional) is often used as a catch all alternative.

The switch statement is executed as follows: The expression is evaluated. If it evaluates to exp_1, statement_1 is executed and the break following the statement terminates the entire switch statement. If expression evaluates to exp_2, statement_2 is executed and the break terminates the switch statement, and soon. If the switch expression does not evaluate to any of the case expressions, control passes to the default case and statement_n is executed and the break terminates the switch statement.

38

Figure 4.4: The switch structure

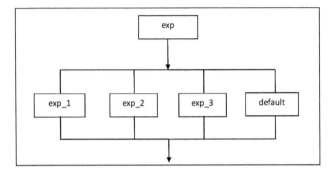

Program 4.3 illustrates the switch statement.

Program 4.3

```
// switch example
#include "pch.h"
#include <iostream>
using namespace std;

void main()
{
        double amount;
        char trans;
        cout << "Enter transaction type (D, W, T): ";
        cin >> trans;
        trans = toupper(trans);  // convert to uppercase
        switch (trans)
        {
            case 'D': cout << "\nDeposit:\n";
                    break;
            case 'W': cout << "\nWithdrawal:\n";
                    break;
            case 'T': cout << "\nTransfer:\n";
                    break;
            default:
                    cout << "\nInvalid transaction!\n";
                    break;
        }
        if (trans == 'D' || trans == 'W' || trans == 'T')
        {
            cout << "Enter amount: ";
            cin >> amount;
            cout << "Amount = " << amount << endl;
        }
}
```

Sample run:

```
Enter transaction type (D, W, T):  T

Transfer:
Enter amount: 555
Amount = 555
```

Program 4.4 is another example.

Program 4.4

```cpp
// select an item from menu
#include "pch.h"
#include <iostream>
using namespace std;

void main()
{
    char selection;
    cout << "\n Menu";
    cout << "\n A - Append";
    cout << "\n M - Modify";
    cout << "\n D - Delete";
    cout << "\n X - Exit";
    cout << "\n\n Enter selection: ";
    cin >> selection;
    selection = toupper(selection);    // convert to uppercase
    switch (selection)
    {
        case 'A':   cout << "\n To append a record\n";
                        break;
        case 'M':   cout << "\n To modify a record\n";
                        break;
        case 'D':   cout << "\n To delete a record\n";
                        break;
        case 'X':   cout << "\n To exit the menu\n";
                        break;
        default:    cout << "\n Invalid selection\n";
    }
}
```

The above program will display the message To append a record, To modify a record, To delete a record, To exit the menu, or Invalid selection depending on the value entered for the prompt Enter selection: A, M, D, X, or some other character.

A block for a case statement may be empty (or null). The code below illustrates this.

```cpp
switch (selection)
{
    case 'A':       // no statement
    case 'M':       // no statement
    case 'D':       cout <<"\n To update a file";
                    break;
    case 'X':       cout <<"\n To exit the menu";
                    break;
    default:        cout <<"\n Invalid selection";
                    break;
}
```

The switch statement differs from the if-else if-else statement in the following ways:

1. The switch permits the execution of more than one alternative (by not putting break statements) whereas the if-else if-else doesn't.

2. A switch performs only equality tests involving integers, characters or string constants whereas if allows you to perform any type of comparison involving any type of data.

4.3 Loops

The **loop** (**repetition** or **iteration**) structure permits the execution of a sequence of instructions repeatedly until a certain condition occurs. This structure comes in three forms: while, do-while, and for.

- **while**

The while structure has the general form

```
while (expression)
{
    statement   // can be a block
}
```

Here, **expression** is evaluated. If it is true the statement is executed; if false, the statement is skipped. Figure 4.5 illustrates this structure.

Figure 4.5: The while structure

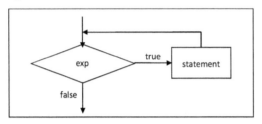

Program 4.5 illustrates this structure. This is an *infinite loop*; the only way to exit the loop is by entering x or X for selection. The break terminates the loop.

Program 4.5

```cpp
#include "pch.h"
#include <iostream>

using namespace std;

void main()
{
    char selection;
    while (true)
    {
        cout << "\n Menu";
        cout << "\n A-Append";
        cout << "\n D-Delete";
        cout << "\n M-Modify";
        cout << "\n X-Exit";
        cout << "\n\n Enter selection: ";
        cin >> selection;
        selection = toupper(selection);
        if (selection == 'X')break;
    }
}
```

41

Output

```
Menu
 A-Append
 D-Delete
 M-Modify
 X-Exit

Enter selection: a

Menu
 A-Append
 D-Delete
 M-Modify
 X-Exit

Enter selection: x
```

- **do-while**

This structure has the general form

```
do
{
    statement
} while (expression);
```

This is similar to the previous structure except that expression is evaluated at the end of the loop. The loop will terminate when the expression evaluates to false. That means, the statement in the do-while loop will execute at least once. Figure 4.6 illustrates this structure.

Figure 4.6: The do-while structure

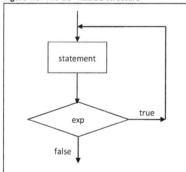

Program 4.6 illustrates the do-while structure. The loop will execute at least once.

Program 4.6

```
#include "pch.h"
#include <iostream>

using namespace std;
```

```
void main()
{
     char selection;
     do
     {
          cout << "\n Menu";
          cout << "\n A-Append";
          cout << "\n D-Delete";
          cout << "\n M-Modify";
          cout << "\n X-Exit";
          cout << "\n\n Enter selection: ";
          cin >> selection;
          selection = toupper(selection);
     } while (selection != 'X');
}
```

Sample run

```
Menu
 A-Append
 D-Delete
 M-Modify
 X-Exit

 Enter selection: d

 Menu
 A-Append
 D-Delete
 M-Modify
 X-Exit

 Enter selection: x
```
The above program displays the menu, then requests a selection. If the selection is 1, 2, or 3, the loop is executed again; otherwise, it is terminated.

▪ **for**

The for structure has the general form

```
for (initialization; test; increment)
{
    statement
}
```

- The initialization part initializes the loop counter (and other variables if needed). This part is performed *only once*, at the start of the loop.

- The test part determines if the loop should continue. If test evaluates to true, the statement (block) is executed; otherwise the loop terminates. This part is performed *every time* at the *beginning* of each loop cycle.

- The increment part increments (or decrements) the loop index (it can also update other variables if needed). This part is performed *every time* at the *end* of each loop cycle.

The execution of the for loop is as follows:

(1) Perform `initialization`.

(2) Evaluate `test`. If the value is `false`, terminate the loop; if the value is `true`, execute the statement.

(3) Perform `increment`.

(4) Go to step (2).

Example

```
for(i=1, sum=0; i<=20; i++)
{
    sum = sum + i;  // {} may be omitted as there is only statement
}

cout << "\nSum of first 20 natural numbers =" << sum;
```

Note that the initialization part in the code has two statements separated by a comma.

Example

```
int i, sum1, sum2;
for(i=2,sum1=0, sum2=0; i<=20; i=i+2)
{
    sum1 = sum1 + i;
    sum2 = sum2 + i*i;
}
cout << "\nSum of first 20 even natural numbers =" << sum1;
cout << "\nSum of their squares = " << sum2;
```

Note: The initial value of loop index doesn't have to be zero and the increment doesn't have to be 1.

Any of the three parts of a `for` loop may be left blank. However, the semicolon (`;`) separating the parts are still required.

Program 4.7 illustrates this loop structure. It calculates student grades.

Program 4.7

```
#include "pch.h"
#include <iostream>
#include <string>

using namespace std;

void main()
{
    string name, grade;
    int i, n = 3, mark;
    for (i = 1; i <= n; i++)
    {
        cout << "\nEnter name: ";
        cin >> name;
        cout << "Enter mark: ";
        cin >> mark;
        if (mark < 50)
            grade = "Fail";
        else
            grade = "Pass";
        cout << name << ", your mark is " << mark << endl;
```

44

```
            cout << "And your grade is " << grade << endl;
        }
}
```

Sample output

```
Enter name: Sally
Enter mark: 77
Sally, your mark is 77
And your grade is Pass

Enter name: Dominic
Enter mark: 50
Dominic, your mark is 50
And your grade is Pass

Enter name: Johnson
Enter mark: 48
Johnson, your mark is 48
And your grade is Fail
```

- **Loop with ranges**

The auto feature in a for loop allows you to access all items in an array or string. It will automatically determine the data type.

Program 4.10 illustrates this. The **auto** feature is used to access and display all elements of array x using a pointer. Auto automatically determines the data type of y. (Arrays are discussed in a later chapter.)

Program 4.10

```
#include "pch.h"
#include <iostream>
#include <string>
using namespace std;

void main()
{
      int x[] = { 1, 2, 3, 4, 5, 6, 7 };

      cout << "\nPrinting integer numbers\n";
      for (auto &y : x)     // access all elements of x using address
            cout << y << "   ";
      cout << endl;
}
```

Output

```
Printing integer numbers
1   2   3   4   5   6   7
```

Program 4.11 is another example. The auto feature is used to display all the elements of arrays of different data types.

Program 4.11

```
#include "pch.h"
#include <iostream>
#include <string>
using namespace std;
```

```
void main()
{
    int  x[] = { 1, 2, 3, 4, 5, 6, 7 };
    float f[] = { 1.1, 2.2, 3.3 };
    string s[] = { "ali", "sam", "wong", "sally" };
    char ch[] = { 'a', 'e', 'i', 'o', 'u' };
    cout << "\nPrinting integer numbers\n";
    for (auto y : x) // auto determines data type of x;
        cout << y << "  ";
    cout << "\nPrinting floating point numbers\n";
    for (auto y : f)
        cout << y << "  ";
    cout << "\nPrinting characters\n";
    for (auto y : ch)
        cout << y << "  ";
    cout << "\nPrinting strings\n";
    for (auto y : s)
        cout << y << "  ";
    cout << endl;
}
```

Output

```
Printing integer numbers
1   2   3   4   5   6   7
Printing floating point numbers
1.1   2.2   3.3
Printing characters
a   e   i   o   u
Printing strings
ali   sam   wong   sally
```

- **Infinite Loops**

We can create an infinite loop by omitting the second expression or using a non-zero constant as in following examples.

Example

```
for( ; ; )
    cout << "\n This is an infinite loop";
```

Example

```
for( ; 1 ; )
    cout << "\n This is an infinite loop";
```

The above statements will display the message This is an infinite loop repeatedly.

To exit from an infinite loop, you must execute a break or return statement as in the code below.

```
for( ; ; )
{
    cout << "\n Menu\n";
    cout << "\n A - Add records";
    cout << "\n M - Modify records";
    cout << "\n D - Delete records";
    cout << "\n X - Exit";
    cout << Select item: ";
```

```
    cin >> selection;
    if(selection == 'X') break;
}
```

The above code will execute repeatedly and display the menu until X is entered for the Select item: prompt.

- **Timing Loops**

The body of a for loop can be empty. In this case, the semicolon at the end terminates the loop.

```
for(delay_time=0; delay_time<20000; delay_time++);
```

This statement will cycle through the loop 20000 times (useful in applications such as music, games, thread and inter-process communication).

- **Nested Loops**

A loop may contain other loops. Such a loop is called a *nested* loop. Program 4.12 is an example of nested loop. It has two for loops with loop indexes i and j. The outer loop index i runs from 1 to 5. And for each value of i, the inner loop index j runs from i+1 to 5.

Program 4.12

```
#include "pch.h"
#include <iostream>
using namespace std;

void main()
{
        int i, j;
        for (i = 1; i < 6; i++)
        {
                cout << "\n" << i;
                for (j = i + 1; j < 6; j++)
                        cout << j;
        }
        cout << "\n";
}
```

Output

```
12345
2345
345
45
5
```

Note that for the last value of i (5), the inner loop is not executed at all. This is because the starting value of j is 6 and the expression j<6 yields false.

4.4 Other Control Flows

C++ also provides jump statements: break, continue, goto and return. These allow program control to be transferred to other parts of a program *unconditionally*.

▪ break

We have already seen how the break statement works in switch, for, while and do-while statements. Executing break in these statements terminate them. The code below illustrates this.

```
// the test part is empty (true)

for(sum=0, count=0 ;  ; count++)
{
   cout << "\nEnter a positive number (-1 to terminate) ";
   cin >> data;
   if (data < 0) break;
   sum = sum + data;
}
```

This is an infinite loop as the test part is blank (which evaluates to true). The only way to exit from the loop is by supplying a negative value for data.

▪ continue

The continue statement (if used) appears inside a for, while or do-while loop. When executed, it transfers control to the *next* loop cycle. Unlike break, the continue statement does not terminate the loop, it simply transfers control to the next loop cycle. The code below illustrates this.

```
for(i=1, sum=0; i<100; i++)
{
   if (i%2) continue;
   sum = sum + i;
}
```

The loop totals even numbers 2, 4, 6, ..., 98 and stores the total in variable sum. If the expression i%2 (remainder of i divided by 2) yields a non-zero value (i.e., if i is odd), the continue statement is executed - starting the next loop cycle. If the remainder is zero (i.e., if i is even), the statement following continue (sum = sum + i) is executed, and the next loop cycle is started.

▪ goto

The goto statement has the form

```
        goto label;
```

where label is any valid C++ identifier. The label however must appear within the same function.

The code below illustrates the goto statement.

```
        sum = 0; i = 0;
        next:         // next is a label
        i++;
        cout << "\nEnter next number: ";
        cin >> data;
        sum += data;
        // Control passes to next if i < 20
        if (i < 20) goto next;
        cout << "\nSum = " << sum;
```

The code prompts the user for data, then adds the value entered to variable sum. If the number of values entered is less than 20, control transfers to the statement following the label next:. Then it increments i, prompts for additional data, and adds it to sum. This is repeated until i reaches the value 20, at which point the value of sum is displayed.

The goto statement is useful in certain situations such as from exiting a deeply nested loop. However, it must be used wisely; otherwise it might produce *unstructured or spaghetti code* that is hard to debug.

▪ return

The return statement has the form

```
return expression;
```

The return statement terminates the execution of a function and passes the value of the expression to the calling function. The value returned must be of the same type as the function type.

A function can have more than one return statement. The execution of the first return statement will terminate the function.

A function is a small program that performs a specific task e.g., calculating the average of a set of numbers or removing embedded blanks in a string. (Functions are discussed in a later chapter.)

Program 4.13 illustrates how a function works. It uses two functions: main() and avg(). The main() function calls avg() to compute average of two floating-point numbers (y1 and y2). It passes arguments y1 and y2 to the corresponding parameters x1 and x2 in avg(). The function computes and returns the average (avgx) to main(). The returned value is assigned to variable avgy and displayed.

Program 4.13

```cpp
#include "pch.h"
#include <iostream>
using namespace std;

void main()
{
    double y1, y2, avgy;
    double avg(double, double);  // prototype
    y1 = 5.5;
    y2 = 7.9;
    cout << "\nAverage = " << avg(y1, y2) << endl;  // calling avg()
    cin.ignore();
}

// Definition of function avg()
double avg(double x1, double x2)
{
    double avgx;       // avgx is a local variable.
    avgx = (x1 + x2) / 2;
    return avgx;       // Returns avgx to main()
}
```

Output

```
Average = 6.7
```

49

A function must declare its type (double, int, float, char, void, etc.) before its name. This information lets the compiler know the data type the function will return to the calling program. In the above program, we have declared avg() as of type double since it will return a floating-point number to main().

Functions need not always return a value. In this case, the function is said to be of type void. Such a function will not have the return expression. In fact you can drop the entire return statement.

4.5 Exceptions

An exception is an error generated when the code behaves in an abnormal way such as when you divide a number by zero, when you access an array element with the loop index exceeds the array size, or when you access a non-existent file.

The try and catch blocks are used for handling exceptions. It takes the form:

```
try
{
    // throw exception
}
catch (type e)
{
    // catch exception
}
```

Here are some examples.

Program 4.14 catches an exception when the denominator is zero.

Program 4.14

```
#include "pch.h"
#include <iostream>
#include <exception>
using namespace std;

int main()
{
    int x = 5, y = 0, z = 1;
    try
    {
        if (y == 0)
            throw y;   // throw exception
        else
            z = x / y;
        cout << z;
    }
    catch (int)
    {
        cout << "Division by zero error.";
    }
    return 0;
}
```

Output

```
Division by zero error.
```

Program 4.15 is similar to the above but uses a function.

Program 4.15

```
#include "pch.h"
#include <iostream>
#include <string>
using namespace std;

int divide(int x, int y)
{
        if (y == 0)
        {
                throw string("Divide by zero");
        }
        return x / y;
}

int main()
{
        try
        {
                cout << "6/2 = " << divide(6, 2) << endl;
                cout << "7/0 invalid: ";
                cout << divide(7, 0) << endl;
        }
        catch (string e)
        {
                cout << e << endl;
        }
        return 0;
}
```

Output

```
6/2 = 3
7/0 invalid: Divide by zero
```

Program 4.16 throws an exception when the array index $i > n$ (6).

Program 4.16

```
#include "pch.h"
#include <iostream>
#include <string>
using namespace std;

int main()
{
        int i, n, x[] = { 1, 2, 3, 4, 5, 6, 7 };

        try
        {
                n = size(x);
                cout << "n= " << n << endl;
                for (i=0; i < 10; i++)
                        if (i >= n)
                                throw string ("Array index out of range.");
                        else
                                cout << "i = " << i << endl;
        }
        catch (string e)
        {
```

51

```
            cout << e << endl;
    }
        return 0;
}
```

Output

```
n= 7
i = 0
i = 1
i = 2
i = 3
i = 4
i = 5
i = 6
Array index out of range.
```

Program 4.17 tests if a character is lowercase, uppercase, digit or control character.

Program 4.17

```
#include "pch.h"
#include <iostream>
#include <string>
using namespace std;

int main()
{
    char ch[] = { 'q', 'W', '9', '\n' };
    int i, n = size(ch);
    for (i = 0; i < n; i++)
    {
        try
        {
            if (islower(ch[i])) throw string("Character is lowercase.");
            if (isupper(ch[i])) throw string("Character is uppercase.");
            if (isdigit(ch[i])) throw string("Character is digit.");
            if (iscntrl(ch[i])) throw string("Character is control
                                            character.");
        }
        catch (string e)
        {
            cout << e << endl;
        }
    }
    return 0;
}
```

Output
```
Character is lowercase.
Character is uppercase.
Character is digit.
Character is control character.
```

4.6 Sample Programs

Program 4.18 uses a switch statement to display the label for selected color code.

Program 4.18

```
#include "pch.h"
#include <iostream>
using namespace std;

void main()
{
    char color;
    cout << "Select color (G, Y, R, X (to exit)): ";
    cin >> color;
    color = toupper(color);
    switch (color)
    {
        case 'G': cout << "\nGo!\n";
                  break;
        case 'Y': cout << "\nWatch!\n";
                  break;
        case 'R': cout << "\nStop!\n";
                  break;
        default:  cout << "\n Invalid color - exiting!\n";
                  break;
    }
}
```

Output

```
Select color (G, Y, R, X (to exit)): g

Go!
```

Program 4.19 uses a for loop to add numbers from 1 to 50 .

Program 4.19

```
#include "pch.h"
#include <iostream>
using namespace std;

void main()
{
    int i, n = 50,  sum = 0;
    for (i = 1; i <= n; i++)
        sum = sum + i;
    cout << "\nSum of integers from 1 to 50 = " << sum << endl;
}
```

Output

```
Sum of integers from 1 to 50 = 1275
```

Program 4.20 uses two for loops to generate a multiplication table. Note that it uses two different loop indexes (i, j) for the loops.

Program 4.20

```
#include "pch.h"
#include <iostream>
#include <iomanip>
using namespace std;

void main()
{
```

```
int i, j, m = 5,  n = 6;
cout << "Multiplication Table\n\n";
cout << "   1  2  3  4  5  6" << "\n\n";
for (i = 1;  i <= m; i++)
{
        cout << i << " ";
        for (j = 1; j <= n; j++)
            cout << setw(3) << i * j;
        cout << "\n";
}
}
```

Output

```
Multiplication Table

    1  2  3  4  5  6

1   1  2  3  4  5  6
2   2  4  6  8 10 12
3   3  6  9 12 15 18
4   4  8 12 16 20 24
5   5 10 15 20 25 30
```

Program 4.21 uses a for loop to generate 50 random numbers in the range [1000, 9999]. The function srand() seeds the random rand() function.

Program 4.21
```
#include "pch.h"
#include <iostream>
#include <iomanip>
using namespace std;

void main()
{
    int i, rn, min = 1000, max = 9999, n = 50;
    srand(time(NULL));  // to seed random number generator
    cout << "Random Numbers:\n";
    for (i = 1; i <= n; i++)
    {
        // generate random number in range
        rn = (rand() % (max - min + 1)) + min;
        cout << setw(5) << rn;
        if (i % 5 == 0) cout << endl;  // display 5 numbers in 1 line
    }
    cout << "\n";
}
```

Output

```
Random Numbers:
 1038  8719  4238  3437  9855
 3797  9365  6285  2450  4612
 6853  2100  2142  1281  3537
 7921  9945  9285  3997  6680
 3976  5891  4655  8906  1457
 2323  2881  3240  1725  6278
 3446  1590  1840  1587  8907
 4237  6611  4617  4456  1867
 3533  7878  2223  9887  5597
 3584  4212  5111  8578  9066
```

Program 4.22 outputs the values in array nums, using a pointer (instead of a loop index). In the first loop iteration, *(nums + dex) points to the first item (given by index 0) in nums (i.e., 92); in the second iteration, it points to the second item in the array (i.e., 81); and so on.

Program 4.22

```
// uses pointers to print values of array
#include "pch.h"
#include <iostream>

using namespace std;

void main()
{
    static int nums[] = { 92, 81, 70, 69, 58 };
    for (int dex = 0; dex < 5; dex++)
        cout << "\n" << *(nums + dex);
    cout << endl;
}
```

Output

```
92
81
70
69
58
```

Program 4.23 reads an arbitrary number of temperature readings into array temp using pointers. Then, it computes the average temperature. The program terminates when the value entered for temperature is 0.

Program 4.23

```
// computes average of temperature readings
#include "pch.h"
#include <iostream>

using namespace std;

void main()
{
    double temp[60], sum = 0.0, *ptr;
    int num, day = 0;
    ptr = temp; // point to array.
    do
    {
        cout << "Enter temperature for day " << ++day;
        cout << "(0 to terminate): ";
        cin >> *ptr;
    } while ((*ptr++) > 0);

    ptr = temp; // reset pointer to array
    num = day - 1;
    for (day = 0; day < num; day++)
        sum += *(ptr++);
    cout << "\nAverage = " << sum / num << endl;
}
```

Sample output

```
Enter temperature for day 1 (0 to terminate): 79.8
```

```
Enter temperature for day 2 (0 to terminate): 56.5
Enter temperature for day 3 (0 to terminate): 67.8
Enter temperature for day 6 (0 to terminate): 0

Average = 68.0
```

Program 4.24 counts the number of occurrences of 'h' in string s.

Program 4.24
```
#include "pch.h"
#include <iostream>
#include <string>

using namespace std;

int main()
{
        string s = "the field of quantum physics";
        int i, count = 0;
        for (i=0; i < s.length(); i++)
        {
                if (s[i] != 'h') continue;
                count = count + 1;
        }
        cout << "No. of h = " << count << endl;
}
```

Output

```
No. of h = 2
```

Program 4.25 produces the same output using the auto feature.

Program 4.25
```
#include "pch.h"
#include <iostream>
#include <string>

using namespace std;

int main()
{
        string s = "the field of quantum physics";
        int i, count = 0;
        for (auto i : s)
        {
                if (i != 'h') continue;
                count = count + 1;
        }
        cout << "No. of h = " << count << endl;
}
```

Output

```
No. of h = 2
```

Exercise

1. What is the purpose of (a) `#include` and (b) `#define` directives in a C++ program?

2. How are functions called from `main()`?

3. Given integer variables a=2, b=5, c=7 and floating-point variables x=10.0, y=10.5, z=20.0. Use type cast to obtain accurate answers for each of the following expressions:

    (a) y + a / b
    (b) a + b (z / a)
    (c) x + (b / a) * c

4. Write suitable declarations, assigning initial values (if any), for each of the following:

    (a) Integer variable: `index`
         Unsigned integer variable: `cust_num`
         Double-precision variables: `gross, tax, net`

    (b) Character variables: `first, last`
         80-element character array: `message`
         One-dimensional character array: `prompt = "ERROR"`
         Character variable: `eol = newline character`

    (c) Floating-point variables: `root1 = 0.007, root2 = -6.8`
         Long integer variable: `big = 781111222`
         Short integer variable: `flag`

5. Write a program that will accept the base and height of a triangle and then calculate and display its `area` with the heading `Area of triangle is ... square meters.`

6. Write a program to read a person's `initial, name, gender` (M = Male, F= Female) and `age` (an integer) and display the same.

7. Write a program that will read an employee's `name, hours_worked` and `rate` and then display the information with his/her pay (to 2 decimal places).

8. XYZ computes the weekly wages of its employees as follows: the rate for the first 40 hours is $5 per hour, the rate for the next 20 hours is $8 per hour and the rate is $10 per hour if the number of hours exceeds 60. The contribution of each employee to SOCSO is 1 percent of the wage earned. Enter the names and hours worked for the company's employees and display their pay slips.

9. Write a program to throw an exception when a string is compared with a floating point number.

10. Given integer variables x and y and a character variable ch. Input values for x, y and ch (the value for ch must be 'a', 'm', 's', 'd' or 'r'). Compute and output the following:

        x + y if ch = 'a'
        x * y if ch = 'm'
        x - y if ch = 's'
        x / y if ch = 'd'
        x % y if ch = 'r'

11. Write programs to print the following patterns:

(a)   (b)

******** $
******* $$$
****** $$$$$
***** $$$$$$$
**** $$$$$$$$$
*** $$$$$$$$$$$
** $$$$$$$$$$$$$
* $$$$$$$$$$$$$$$

12. Trace the output for the below.

```
#include "pch.h"
#include <iostream>
using namespace std;

void main()
{
    int i, n, x[] = { 33, 11, 66, 99, 44, 22, 88 };
    n = size(x);
    for (i = n - 1; i >= 0; i--)
        cout << x[i] << "   ";
}
```

Chapter 5

Built-in Functions

Learning Outcomes:

After completing this chapter, the student will be able to

- *Explain C++ header files.*
- *Explain standard built-in library functions.*
- *List some categories of functions.*
- *Use functions in programs.*

5.1 Header Files

Visual C++ provides several **precompiled header files** containing commonly used functions which you can freely use without having to write code for them. These are called *built-in* or *standard library functions*.

Each header file contains functions related to a specific category. For example, the header file `string` contains functions for processing strings such as for taking the length of a string. Similarly, the header file `iostream` contains functions for performing input/output operations using `cin >>` and `cout <<` respectively.

Visual C++ also provides a special **pre**compiled header file **pch.h**. This header file is required to run all C++ programs and must be placed ***before*** the other header files. It contains most of the basic functions needed to run C++ programs. (Earlier versions may use the header file: **st**andard **a**pplication **f**ramework e**x**tensions **stdafx.h**)

To use header files, you need to declare them using the `#include` directive. The directive begins with a sharp sign (#) and the keyword `include` followed by the name of the header file. The directive tells the compiler to include the functions contained in the header file.

The `#include` directives take the form

```
#include "pch.h"    // this header file must come first
#include <string>
#include <iostream>
```

Include only the header files your application needs.

As C++ is a superset of the C language, it also lets you include header files from the C language which have the file extension `.h`. C++ allows you to use both C and C++ header files. To avoid conflict, C++ header files usually begins with the letter 'c' as in `<cstdio>` and `<cctype>` (C uses `<stdio>` and `<ctype>`.

5.2 Categories of Header Files

Visual C++ provides many categories of header files. Each category contains functions for performing specific tasks such as for input/output or for processing strings.

Here, we will list and discuss only a few of these categories and header files. For a complete list, you need to consult the C++ documentation.

Categories of header files

Category	Headers
Algorithms	`<algorithm>`
C library wrappers	`<cassert>`, `<cctype>`, `<cerrno>`, `<cfenv>`, `<cfloat>`, `<cinttypes>`, `<ciso646>`, `<climits>`, `<clocale>`, `<cmath>`, `<csetjmp>`, `<csignal>`, `<cstdarg>`, `<cstdbool>`, `<cstddef>`, `<cstdint>`, `<cstdio>`, `<cstdlib>`, `<cstring>`, `<ctgmath>`, `<ctime>`, `<cwchar>`, `<cwctype>`
I/O and formatting	`<filesystem>`, `<fstream>`, `<iomanip>`, `<ios>`, `<iosfwd>`, `<iostream>`, `<istream>`, `<ostream>`, `<sstream>`, `<streambuf>`, `<strstream>`
Errors and exception handling	`<exception>`, `<stdexcept>`, `<system_error>`
Strings and character data	`<regex>`, `<string>`
Math and numerical	`<complex>`, `<limits>`, `<numeric>`, `<random>`, `<ratio>`, `<valarray>`
Sequence containers	`<array>`, `<deque>`, `<forward_list>`, `<list>`, `<vector>`
Adaptor containers	`<queue>`, `<stack>`

5.3 Functions in Header Files

In this section, we will look at some functions in some of the header files.

pch.h

The precompiled header file `pch.h` (or `stdafx.h` if you are using an earlier version) contains basic functions needed to run C++ programs. If your application requires other categories of functions, you need to include the appropriate header files.

<iostream>

The `<iostream>` header file contains `cin >>` and `cout <<` for performing input/output. The `cin >>` is used for reading input data from the keyboard while the `cout <<` is used for sending output to the monitor. Note the direction of the input/output operators >> and <<. The `cin.ignore()` function simply skips the rest of characters in the input buffer.

Program 5.1 illustrates some functions in this header file.

Program 5.1

```
// illustrates <iostream> functions
#include "pch.h"
#include <iostream>
#include <string>
using namespace std;
```

```
void main()
{
    string name;
    int age;
    cout << "Enter name: ";  // output
    cin >> name;        // input
    cout << "Enter age: ";
    cin >> age;
    cout <<"\n" << name << ", your age is " << age << endl;
    cin.ignore();
}
```

Sample output

```
Enter name: Sam
Enter age: 29

Sam, your age is 29
```

<iomanip>

The <iomanip> header file contains formatting functions such as setw(), setprecision() and
fixed. These are useful for *formatting* output. For example, you can use the function setw(n) to print
your results in n columns.

Program 5.2 illustrates this (and other) header files. The input/output functions - setw(),
setprecision() and fixed - are used for formatting output.

Program 5.2

```
// illustrates formatting output using <iomanip> header file
#include "pch.h"
#include <iostream>
#include <string>
#include <iomanip>      // header for setting width and precision
using namespace std;

void main()
{
    string name = "Sally Nelson";
    int x = 12345;
    double y = 123.45678;
    cout << "Name: " << setw(12) << name << endl;
    cout << "Name: " << setw(17) << name << endl;
    cout << "x = : " << setw(7) << x << endl;
    cout << "x = : " << setw(10) << x << endl;
    cout << setprecision(6) << "y = " << y << endl;
    cout << setprecision(8) << "y = " << y << endl;
    cout << fixed;
    cout << name <<"\t" << x << "\t" << y << endl;
}
```

Output

```
Name: Sally Nelson
Name:     Sally Nelson
x = :  12345
x = :      12345
y = 123.457
y = 123.45678
Sally Nelson    12345    123.45678000
```

\<string\>

The \<string\> header file has contains string and character processing functions such as get (), put (), getline (), size (), find () and substr ().

Programs 5. 3 and 5.4 illustrate some of the functions in this file.

Program 5.3 reads and prints characters and strings. Note the character handling functions get (ch) and put (ch) for reading and writing characters. The cin.ignore () function skips the rest of characters in the input buffer.

Program 5.3

```cpp
#include "pch.h"
#include <iostream>
#include <string>
using namespace std;

void main()
{
    char ch;
    string word, line;
    cout << "Type a character: ";
    cin.get(ch);
    cout << "Character read is: " << ch << endl;
    cout << "\nType another character: ";
    cin >> ch;
    cout << "Character read is: ";
    cout.put(ch);
    cout << "\n\nConstant literal: ";
    cout.put('y');
    cout << endl;
    cout << "\nType a word: ";
    cin >> word;   // will only read the first word
    cout << "Word read is: " << word << endl;
    cin.ignore();   // this clears the buffer
    cout << "\nType a line: ";
    getline(cin, line);
    cout << "\nLine read is: " << line << endl;
}
```

Output

```
Type a character: w
Character read is: w

Type another character: q
Character read is: q

Constant literal: y

Type a word: nice
Word read is: nice

Type a line: nice day today

Line read is: nice day today
```

Program 5.4 illustrates string processing. It performs several string functions such as size (), length (), substr (), find (), and insert ().

Program 5.4
```
// illustrates string functions
#include "pch.h"
#include <iostream>
#include <string>
using namespace std;

void main()
{
    string s = "Quantum physics changes our understanding of reality!";
    cout << "String : " << s << endl;
    // returns number of characters in string
    cout << "Length = " << size(s) << endl;  // using size
    cout << "Length = " << s.length() << endl;  // using length

    cout << "Position of first blank space: " << s.find(' ') << endl;
    cout << "Substring from position 8 to 20: " << s.substr(8, 20) << endl;

    // return last character
    cout << "Last character: " << s.back() << endl;
    cout << "Position of physics from beginning: " <<
            s.find_first_of("physics") << endl;
    cout << "Position of physics from end: " << s.find_last_of("physics")
         << endl;
    cout << "Replace 7 characters from position 8: " <<
            s.replace(8, 7, "mechanics") << endl;
    cout << "Insert string from position 8: " << s.insert(8, "physics or ")
         << endl;
}
```

Output

```
String : Quantum physics changes our understanding of reality!
Length = 53
Length = 53
Position of first blank space: 7
Substring from position 8 to 20: physics changes our
Last character: !
Position of physics from beginning: 8
Position of physics from end: 51
Replace 7 chars from position 8: Quantum mechanics changes our understanding of
reality!
Insert string from position 8: Quantum physics or mechanics changes our
understanding of reality!
```

`<ctime>`

The `<ctime>` header file contains timer functions such as now.

Program 5.5 uses `srand(time(NULL))` to seed the random number generator. It also uses several math functions such as `sqrt()`, `log()`, `exp()`, `pow()`, `round()` and `fmax()` and `fmin()` (floating point max and min).

Program 5.5
```
#include "pch.h"
#include <iostream>
#include <ctime>
using namespace std;

int main()
```

```
{
    double d1 = 225, d2 = 7;
    int x = 2, y = 3;
    srand((time(NULL)));   // time needs <ctime>
    cout << "Square root of " << d1 << " = " << sqrt(d1) << endl;
    cout << "Log of " << d2 << " = " << log(d2) << endl;
    cout << "2^3 = " << pow(x, y) << endl;
    cout << "e^3 = " << exp(y) << endl;
    cout << "Round 227/7 = " << round(d1/d2) << endl;
    cout << "Max(225, 7) = " << fmax(d1, d2) << endl;
    cout << "Sine of 0.7 = " << sin(0.7) << endl;
    cout << "Random number: " << rand()/10000 << endl;
    cout << "Round (sqrt(227/7)) = " << round(sqrt(d1 / d2)) << endl;
    cout << "Sqrt(min(225, 7)) = " << sqrt(fmin(d1, d2)) << endl;
}
```

Output

```
Square root of 225 = 15
Log of 7 = 1.94591
2^3 = 8
e^3 = 20.0855
Round 227/7 = 32
Max(225, 7) = 225
Sine of 0.7 = 0.644218
Random number: 2
Round (sqrt(227/7)) = 6
Sqrt(min(225, 7)) = 2.64575
```

`<array>`

The `<array>` header file contains functions for comparing and testing arrays (element by element).

Program 5.6 tests if two arrays are equal (element by element), less than, or great than equal.

Program 5.6

```
#include "pch.h"
#include <iostream>
#include <array>
using namespace std;

int main()
{
    int x[5] = { 1, 2, 3, 4, 5 };
    int y[5] = { 55, 44, 33, 22, 11 };
    int z[5] = { 1, 2, 3, 4, 5 };
    if (x == y)  // test array equality
        cout << "Array x = array y.\n";
    else
        cout << "Array x != array y.\n";
    if (y <= x)
        cout << "Array y <= array x.\n";
    if (x == z)
        cout << "Array x = array z.\n";
    if (y > z)
        cout << "Array y > array z.\n";
}
```

Output

64

```
Array x != array y.
Array y <= array x.
Array y > array z.
```

\<fstream\>

The \<fstream\> header file contains functions for reading input data from and writing output to text files. To perform input/output, it uses the file streams ifstream and ofstream.

Program 5.7 opens a text file (mark.txt) using the file streams ifstream object infile. Then it uses the infile for testing, reading and closing the file.

Program 5.7

```
#include "pch.h"
#include <iostream>
#include <fstream>   // needed for input/output on text files
#include <string>
using namespace std;

void main()
{
      string line;
      ifstream infile;   // declare object for ifstream

      infile.open("C:\\Users\\Sellappan\\Desktop\\mark.txt");

      if (!infile)
      {
            cout << "Cannot open file!\n";
            exit(1);
      }

      while (getline(infile, line))
      {
            cout << line << endl;
      }
      infile.close();   // close file stream
}
```

Input file

Output

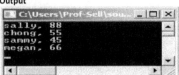

65

<chrono>

This header file contains functions related to the system clock such as `now()`, `count()` and `duration_cast`.

Program 5.8 calculates the elapsed time for completing a long loop with no statements. Note that it uses the `chrono::high_resolution_clock` and the `duration_cast` and the functions `now()` and `count()`.

Program 5.8

```
// calculating elapsed time
#include "pch.h"
#include <iostream>
#include <chrono>  // needs this header
using namespace std;

void main()
{
    auto started = chrono::high_resolution_clock::now();
    for (int i = 0; i < 5000000; i++) {}
    auto done = chrono::high_resolution_clock::now();
    cout << "Elapsed time = ";
    cout << chrono::duration_cast<chrono::milliseconds>(done -
        started).count();
    cout << endl;
}
```

Output

```
Elapsed time = 9
```

5.3 Sample Programs

Program 5.9 illustrates character-testing functions. The functions `isupper()` and `islower()` test whether a letter is uppercase or lowercase. The function `isdigit()` tests whether a character is a digit while the function `tolower()` converts an uppercase letter to lowercase.

Program 5.9

```
// illustrates character functions
#include "pch.h"    // pch includes character functions
#include <iostream>
using namespace std;

void main()
{
    char ch = 'A';
    if (isupper(ch))
        cout << ch << " is an uppercase letter\n";
    else
        cout << ch << " is not an uppercase letter\n";
    if (isdigit(ch))
        cout << ch << " is a digit\n";
    else
        cout << ch << " is not a digit\n";
    ch = tolower(ch);
    if (islower(ch))
```

66

```
            cout << ch << " is a lowercase letter\n";
      else
            cout << ch << " is not a lowercase letter\n";
}
```

Output

```
A is an uppercase letter
A is not a digit
a is a lowercase letter
```

Program 5.10 generates n=10 integer random numbers in the range [min, max], i.e. [555, 5555] It seeds the random number generator using the time () function contained in the header file <ctime>.

Program 5.10

```
#include "pch.h"
#include <iostream>
#include <ctime>
#define n 10

using namespace std;

void main()
{
      int i, min = 555, max = 5555, rn;
      char ch;
      srand(time(NULL));
      cout << "Random numbers in the range[555, 5555]:\n";
      for (i = 0; i < n; i++)
      {
            rn = (rand() % (max + 1 - min)) + min;
            cout << rn << "  ";
      }
      cout << endl;
}
```

Output

```
Random numbers in the range [555, 5555]:
3856   1323   4090   4674   3960   1825   2141   1707   3851   5303
```

Program 5.11 generates n=10 integer random numbers in the range [min, max] in array x [ ], and also counts how many of these are even/odd.

Program 5.11

```
#include "pch.h"
#include <iostream>
#include <ctime>
#define n 10
using namespace std;

void main()
{
      int i, odd = 0, even = 0, min = 555, max = 5555, x[n];
      srand(time(NULL));
      cout << "Random numbers:" << endl;
      for (i = 0; i < n; i++)
      {
            x[i] = (rand() % (max + 1 - min)) + min;
            if (x[i] % 2 == 0)
```

```
                    even++;
            else
                    odd++;
            cout << x[i] << "   ";
        }
        cout << "\nNo.of even numbers = " << even << endl;
        cout << "No.of odd numbers = " << odd << endl;
}
```

Output

```
Random numbers:
5074  2781  5520  1858  2437  1937  3441  3942  2291  833
No.of even numbers = 4
No.of odd numbers = 6
```

Program 5.12 uses the <sstream> header file. The stringstream parses a line of characters to extract tokens (delimited by ' '). The ss is used as a temporary string variable to perform this task.

Program 5.12

```
#include "pch.h"
#include <iostream>
#include <string>
#include <sstream>  // string stream
using namespace std;

void main()
{
        int count = 0;
        string token, line = "time and tide wait for no man";
        stringstream ss(line);  // ss is a string variable
        cout << "Line: " << line << "\n\n";
        while (getline(ss, token, ' '))  // tokenize on ' '
        {
                cout << token << endl;
                count = count + 1;
        }
        cout << "\nNo. of tokens = " << count << endl;
}
```

Output
```
time
and
tide
wait
for
no
man

No. of tokens = 7
```

Program 5.13 is similar to the above program but it receives the input string from the console. Note the function getline(cin, line, '\n'); also removes the new line character (\n).

Program 5.13

```
#include "pch.h"
#include <iostream>
#include <string>
#include <sstream>
using namespace std;
```

```
void main()
{
    int count = 0;
    string token, line;
    cout << "Enter a line: ";
    getline(cin, line, '\n'); // read a line, remove \n
    stringstream ss(line);
    cout << "\nTokens are: \n";
    while (getline(ss, token, ' '))
    {
        cout << token << endl;
        count = count + 1;
    }
    cout << "\nNo. of tokens = " << count << endl;
}
```

Output

```
Enter a line: small is beautiful

Tokens are:
small
is
beautiful

No. of tokens = 3
```

Program 5.14 is similar to Program 5.13, but extracts the string tokens differently – using the functions `length()`, `find()` and `substr()`.

Program 5.14

```
#include "pch.h"
#include <iostream>
#include <string>
using namespace std;

void main()
{
    string s2, s = "quantum physics changes understanding of reality";
    int n, pos;
    cout << "String: " << s << endl;
    n = s.length();
    cout << "Length = " << n << endl;
    cout << "Tokens:" << endl;
    while (n > 0)
    {
        pos = s.find(' ');   // fins first blank
        if (pos > 0)
        {
            s2 = s.substr(0, pos);   // get the first word in s
            cout << s2 << endl;
            s = s.substr(pos + 1);   // copy rest of string to end
            n = s.length();
        }
        else
        {
            cout << s << endl;   // print last word
            break;
        }
    }
}
```

Output

```
String: quantum physics changes understanding of reality
Length = 48
Tokens:
quantum
physics
changes
understanding
of
reality
```

Program 5.15 removes all embedded blanks/spaces in a string.

Program 5.15

```
#include "pch.h"
#include <iostream>
#include <string>
using namespace std;

void main()
{
        string s = "quantum physics changes our understanding of reality";

        int n, pos;
        cout << "String: " << s << endl;
        pos = s.find(' ');
        while (pos > 0)
        {
                s = s.substr(0, pos) + s.substr(pos + 1);
                cout << s << endl;
                pos = s.find(' ');
        }
}
```

Output

```
String: quantum physics changes our understanding of reality
quantumphysics changes our understanding of reality
quantumphysicschanges our understanding of reality
quantumphysicschangesour understanding of reality
quantumphysicschangesourunderstanding of reality
quantumphysicschangesourunderstandingof reality
quantumphysicschangesourunderstandingofreality
```

Exercise

1. Write a program to count the number of occurrences of character 'a' in a string.

2. Write a program to generate 50 integer random numbers in the range [777, 7777]. How many of these are divisible by 7?

3. Write a program to format the floating point numbers d1 = 0.000789, d2 = 1.2345 and d3 = 789.12345 to two decimal places. Display the same in 7 columns.

4. Given x = 5, y = 3, p = 123.45, q = 543.12345, write a program to calculate x^y, `log(p)`, `sqrt (q)` and `exp(y)` and `log(sqrt(p+q))`.

5. Write a program to read and write characters input from the console.

6. Write a program to read a string from the console and count the number of tokens in it.

7. Write a program to convert a string from uppercase to lowercase and vice versa.

Chapter 6

User-defined Functions

Learning Outcomes:

After completing this chapter, the student will be able to

- *Explain function types.*
- *Declare function prototypes.*
- *Define and call functions.*
- *Call function as statement/expression.*
- *Pass parameters by value/reference.*
- *Call functions using pointers.*
- *Write program using functions.*

In addition to using built-in library functions, you can also define your own functions. These are called user-defined or programmer-defined functions. You can define as many functions as your program needs.

You can also write, compile and tore functions in a header file and later include this file in your program just like other header files. To do this, you include a directive such as (where `myfile.h` is your header file):

```
#include "myfile.h" // programmer-created header files
                     // are enclosed with ""
void main()
{
   .
   .
   .
}
```

A function may call other functions which in turn can call yet other functions. A function may also call itself recursively.

Functions must specify their type such as `int, string, void, double, string`. This is the data type that the function will receive from the calling function via the `return` statement.

We will discuss these and other topics in this chapter.

6.1 Defining Functions

Before you can use a function, you must define it. A function definition takes the form

```
return_type function_name (parameter-list)
{
   variable declaration
   statements
```

```
    return expression
}
```

where
- `return_type` is any valid C++ data type
- `function_name` is any valid C++ identifier
- `parameter-list` is a list of parameters separated by commas
- `variable declaration` is a list of variables declared in the function
- `return` is a C++ keyword
- `expression` is the value returned by the function

The `return_type` before the `function_name` tells the data type the function will receive when the `return` statement is executed in the called program. The `return` value can be any valid data type such as `int`, `double`, `void`, `char`, etc.

If a function does not return a value to the calling function it is said to be of type `void`. If the return type is `void`, the `return` statement may be dropped altogether.

The `parameter-list` contains the list of parameters separated by commas. The parameters must also have type specification. The type tells the data type the parameter will pass to the calling function.

The `parameter-list` takes the form

```
    type var_1, type var_2, ..., type var_n
```

6.2 Passing Arguments to Functions

The variables declared in a function are *local* to that function, i.e., they have local scope, visible only within the function. Other functions can use the same variable names but their scope will be local to them.

The calling function passes **arguments** (sometimes called parameters) to the called function. The called function receives and stores these values in its **parameters** which are local to the function (unless called by reference). The parameters act as inputs to the function. The *number* and *type* of arguments passed by the calling function must be the same as the number and type of the parameters in the called function.

The code below illustrates how arguments are passed to a function. The `main()` function passes the argument x (12) to the `prt()` function which is then stored in parameter y which is displayed.

Note that we have used different names for argument x in `main()` and parameter y in `prt()`. You can also give the same name and the result would be identical. This is because parameter x (if y is replaced by x) is local to the function and therefore not visible to `main()`. Any change made to x in `prt()` will not change the value of x in `main()` because they both have different scopes.

Note: If the called function appears *after* the calling function, the calling function must declare a ***prototype*** for the called function. This tells the compiler that the function referenced is defined later in the program.

The value 12 is passed from main() to prt()

```
#include <iostream>

void prt(int);    // prototype as its definition appears after main()
```

```
void main()
{
    int = 12;
    prt(x);          // calls prt() and passes x
}

void prt(int y)     // prt() function definition
{
    cout << y;
}
```

When a function calls another function, it passes control to the called function. When the called function terminates, it control returns back to the calling function as the code below shows. The arrows show the flow of control between `main()` and `another()`. The `main()` calls `another()`; upon termination, `another()` returns control back to `main()`.

Flow of control between main() and another()

```
void main()
{
    . . .
    another();              // Calls another()
    . . .
}

void another()
{
    . . .
    return;                 // Returns to main()
}
```

6.3 Calling Functions

A function call consists of the name of the function followed by a list of arguments whose values are to be passed to the corresponding parameters in the called function. The number and type of the arguments must correspond to the number and type of the parameters in the called function.

A function call may take the form of a single statement (the return type must be `void`) or as an expression in an assignment or output statement (with return type `int`, `double`, `string`, etc).

- **Function Call as Statement**

Program 6.1 illustrates function call as a statement. The `main()` function calls the function `display_wage()` and passes the two arguments `rate` and `hours`.

```
display_wage(rate, hours);
```
The called function `display_wage()` receives the arguments and stores them in its parameters `prate` and `phours`.

```
void display_wage(double prate, int phours);
```

Note that arguments `rate` and `hours` are local to `main()` while the parameters `prate` and `phours` are local to `display_wage()`.

Program 6.1

```
// illustrates function call as statement
#include "pch.h"
#include <iostream>
#include <string>
using namespace std;

void main()
{
      void display_wage(double, int); // function prototype
      double rate = 77.00;
      int hours = 35;
      display_wage(rate, hours); // call display_wage
}

void display_wage(double prate, int phours)
{
      cout << "Wage = $";
      cout << prate * (double)phours;
}
```

Output

```
Wage = $2695
```

When main() calls display_wage(), the following actions take place:

- The arguments rate and hours in main() are passed to the corresponding parameters prate and phours in display_wage().

- The function display_wage() executes using the values in prate and phours. It computes and displays the wage (prate*phours). It does not return any value to main().

Only a *copy* of the arguments are passed to the parameters in the called function. We say the arguments are **passed by value**. What occurs inside the called function will have no effect on the arguments in the calling function. Any change in prate or phours will not have any effect on rate or hours as the arguments and parameters both have different scope.

Note that main() function declares the prototype

```
      void display_wage(double, int);
```

This is because main() calls display_wage() which appears after main(). The C++ compiler needs this information before it can compile. The prototype provides that information. We can avoid the prototype by placing display_wage() before main().

The void function type tells the compiler that it doesn't return any value to the calling program. In this case, we can drop the return statement as in the above program.

- **Function Call as Expression**

You can also call a function within an expression in an assignment statement or in an output statement. Program 6.2 illustrates this.

The value 15 is passed to parameter y of square(). When the assignment statement y = y * y; is executed, the value of y changes to 225 which is then returned to `main()`. The value of x (15) remains unchanged since only a copy of x is passed to y.

Program 6.2

```
// illustrates function call as expression
#include "pch.h"
#include <iostream>
#include <string>
using namespace std;

int square(int y)
{
    y = y * y;
    return y;
}

void main()
{
    int xsq, x = 15;
    cout << "x = " << x;
    xsq = square(x); // function call as expression
    cout << "\nSquare of x = " << xsq;
    // calling in output statement
    cout << "\nSquare of x = " << square(x) << endl;


}
```

Output

```
x = 15
Square of x = 225
Square of x = 225
```

6.4 Returning Values

A function may or may not return a value to the calling function. If a function does not return a value, it is said to be of type `void`. A `void` type function does not have any expression part in the `return` statement. In fact, the `return` statement itself can be dropped.

If a function returns a value, its value is given by the expression following the `return` statement. A function may be called any number of times as Program 6.3 illustrates.

Program 6.3

```
// convert lowercase character to upper case
#include "pch.h"
#include <iostream>
#include <string>
using namespace std;

void main()
{
    char lower, upper;
    char lower_to_upper(char); // prototype
    cout << "Please enter a lower-case character: ";
    cin >> lower;
    upper = lower_to_upper(lower);
    cout << "\nThe upper-case equivalent is " << upper << endl;
```

76

```
}
char lower_to_upper(char c1)
// programmer-defined conversion function
{
     char c2;
     // uses immediate if operator ?
     c2 = (c1 >= 'a' && c1 <= 'z') ? ('A' + c1 - 'a') : c1;
     return(c2);
}
```

Sample output

```
Please enter a lower-case character: q

The upper-case equivalent is Q
```

Here, main() calls lower_to_upper() by passing character argument lower to the parameter c1.
The lower_to_upper() converts the lowercase character to uppercase and passes it to main() via the
return statement.

The statement before the return statement needs some explanation.

The statement uses the *immediate if* operator ? in the expression. This operator takes the form

     x ? y : z

where x, y and z represent valid C++ expressions. The expression yields the value y if x is true (any non-
zero value) or the value z if x is false (or zero).

Thus the statement assigns the value of the expression ('A'+c1-'a') to c2 if the value of (c1>'a' &&
c1<='z') is true and the value of the expression c1 if it is false.

6.5 Function Prototypes

We have already seen function prototypes earlier. A function prototype specifies the name and type of
function and number and type of parameters. It supplies this information to the complier so that it can
compile the program correctly. It is only needed if the function that requires it appears before it.

The function prototype declaration has the general form

     type function_name (parameter_1 type, parameter_2 type, ...,
                          type parameter_n type);

Program 6.4 illustrates function prototype.

Program 6.4

```
// Program to illustrate function prototype
#include "pch.h"
#include <iostream>
using namespace std;

void main()
{
     void sum(int, int); // function prototype
```
77

```
      int a = 2, b = 3;
      cout << "a = " << a;
      cout << "\nb = " << b;
      sum(a, b);   // calls sum() to compute and display sum
      cin.ignore();
}

void sum(int c, int d)
{
      cout << "\nSum = " << c + d;
}
```

Output

```
a = 2
b = 3
Sum = 5
```

6.6 Passing Arguments by Reference

In our examples, the calling function passed arguments to the corresponding parameters in the called function. The called function then used these parameter values to do its task. Any changes made to these parameters in the called function did not have any effect on the arguments in the calling function as only copies are passed. This way of passing arguments is called **passing by value**.

There may be times where the calling function may want the called function to change the argument values. How can we do this?

C++ allows you to pass arguments by reference – that is, by passing their *addresses*. In this case, when the called function changes the parameter values, it effectively changes the argument values as they refer to the same memory location. Both the arguments and parameters are the same – they both operate on the same variable even if they have different names. This is called **passing by reference**.

To pass an argument by reference, you need to insert the *address of* operator & to the function parameter type.

Program 6.5 illustrates this. The max_min() function has four parameters - two of type int and two pointers to type int. The main() passes four arguments to max_min(); the first two (x and y) are passed by value while the last two are passed by reference. The function calculates the maximum and minimum of x and y and stores the results in max and min. The addresses of max and min in both functions are the same.

Program 6.5

```
#include "pch.h"
#include <iostream>
using namespace std;

// x and y are value parameters; max and min are reference parameters
void max_min(int x, int y, int& max, int& min)
{
      if (x > y)
            max = x;   // max in main is changed
      else
            max = y;
      if (x < y)
            min = x;
      else
```

78

```
        min = y;
}

void main()
{
    char ch;
    int x, y, min, max;
    cout << "\nEnter two numbers: ";
    cin >> x >> y;
    max_min(x, y, max, min);
    cout << "\nMaximum = " << max << endl;
    cout << "\nMinimum = " << min << endl;
}
```

Output

```
Enter two numbers: 5 7

Maximum = 7
Minimum = 5
```

Program 6.6 illustrates passing arguments by reference. It passes addresses of variables (&x and &y). The program swaps the contents of two integer variables.

Program 6.6

```
#include "pch.h"
#include <iostream>

using namespace std;

void int_swap(int *x, int *y) // parameters here are pointers
{
    int temp;
    temp = *x;   // save the value of address x
    *x = *y;     // put y into x
    *y = temp;   // put x into y
}


void main()
{
    int x = 10, y = 20;
    cout << "\nInitial values of x and y are: ";
    cout << x << " and " << y;
    int_swap(&x, &y); // addresses of x and y are passed
    cout << "\nSwapped values of x and y are: ";
    cout << x << " and " << y;
    cout << endl;
}
```

Output

```
Initial values of x and y are: 10 and 20
Swapped values of x and y are: 20 and 10
```

C++ passes strings and arrays by reference. This is because making local copies of these data structures can be inefficient/time-consuming.

6.7 Passing Pointers to Functions

Pointers can also be used to access functions. To do this, you prefix the pointer with the function type (`int`, `double`, `char`, `void`). You also need to specify the parameters and their types. For example, a pointer to a function with floating-point parameters and which returns a floating-point value would be declared as follows:

```
double (*ptr) (double, double);
```

This declaration is similar to an ordinary function declaration in that you have the function type as well as the parameter list. However, instead of the function name, you have a function pointer (`*ptr`). Note that the function pointer must be enclosed in parentheses.

To illustrate, let's suppose the above pointer points to the function `minimum()` with two parameters of type `double`. To access this function, you assign the address of the function to the pointer as follows:

```
ptr = &minimum;
```

Then you can call the function by using the pointer `ptr`.

Program 6.7 illustrates accessing function using a pointer. The statement

```
double (*ptr)(double, double);
```

specifies two parameters of type `double`. Note that instead of the function name, the prototype uses a pointer. The statement

```
ptr = &minimum;
```

assigns the address of `minimum()` to `ptr`.

The statement

```
small = (*ptr)(x1, x2)
```

calls the function pointed to by (`*ptr`), i.e., function `minimum()` which then returns the smaller of the two values.

Program 6.7

```
// illustrates pointer to function
#include "pch.h"
#include <iostream>
using namespace std;

void main()
{
    double minimum(double, double);      // prototype
    double (*ptr)(double, double);  // (*ptr) is pointer to function
    double x1, x2, small;
    ptr = &minimum;              // assign address of minimum to ptr
    cout << "\nEnter 2 numbers: ";
    cin >> x1 >> x2;
    small = (*ptr)(x1, x2);          // call function pointed to by ptr.
    cout << "\nSmaller of the two is " << small << endl;
}
```

```
double minimum(double y1, double y2)
{
    if (y1 < y2) return y1;
    else return y2;
}
```

Sample output

```
Enter 2 numbers: 112.6   86.7
Smaller of the two is 86.7
```

C++ also lets you pass a function as an argument. Program 6.8 illustrates this. The program uses three functions – minimum(), maximum(), get_answer() – in addition to main(). The main() function declares a pointer (*ptr) to a function of a type double which has two parameters (of type double). The main() function then assigns the address of function minimum() or maximum() to function ptr depending on the input (s or b) supplied to variable request. The program then calls get_answer() to execute the intended function. Finally, it displays the contents of answer. Note that the program uses only one function pointer in the prototype to reference minimum() or maximum().

Program 6.8

```
// illustrates passing function to another function
#include "pch.h"
#include <iostream>
using namespace std;

void main()
{
    double mini(double, double); // prototype
    double maxi(double, double); // prototype
    double get_answer(double (*)(double, double), double, double);
    double(*ptr) (double, double); // (*ptr)is a pointer
    double x1, x2, answer;
    char request;
    cout << "\nEnter 2 numbers: ";
    cin >> x1 >> x2;
    cout << "\nEnter code (S - smaller, B - bigger): ";
    cin >> request;
    request = toupper(request);
    if (request == 'S')
        ptr = &mini;        // ptr to mini()
    else
        ptr = &maxi;        // ptr to maxi()

    // first argument is a function pointer
    answer = get_answer(ptr, x1, x2);
    cout << "\nAnswer = " << answer << endl;
}

double mini(double y1, double y2)
{
    if (y1 < y2)
        return y1;
    else
        return y2;
}

double maxi(double y1, double y2)
{
    if (y1 > y2)
        return y1;
    else
```

```
            return y2;
}
// function has three parameters, first is a pointer to function
double get_answer(double (*ptr)(double, double), double y1, double y2)
{
      double answer;
      // calls mini()or maxi() depending on request
      answer = (*ptr)(y1, y2);
      return answer;
}
```

Sample output

```
Enter 2 numbers: 77 22

Enter code (S - smaller, B - bigger): s

Answer = 22
```

Program 6.9 is another example. The main() function calls the function addcon() with two pointer arguments: the first points to variable x and the second points to variable y. The addcon() function then uses the addresses received from main() to get the values stored in x and y. Then it increments their values by 10 and stores the results back in the same memory locations. Upon execution, x will have the value 16, and y the value 17.

Program 6.9

```
// function reads a value from the calling program's address,
// adds a constant, and returns the result to same spot
#include "pch.h"
#include <iostream>
using namespace std;

void main()
{
      int x = 6, y = 7;
      int addcon(int*, int*);
      addcon(&x, &y);
      cout << "\nFirst is " << x << ", second is " << y << endl;
}

int addcon(int *px, int *py)
{
      *px = *px + 10;
      *py = *py + 10;
      return (*px, *py);
}
```

Output

```
First is 16, second is 17
```

6.8 Macro & Inline Functions

If a program requires the same sequence of steps in several places, you can write a function and call it wherever it is needed. Executing a function call however may take more overhead as it requires stack operations.

Another way is to insert the sequence of steps wherever they are needed in the program. This will increase the program size and memory requirement. Is there a better way?

You will normally use a function if the sequence of steps is long. If the sequence is short, you can use a *macro* or *inline function*. The macro and inline function will automatically substitute the code wherever the macro name and inline function appear in the program.

Macros

You define a macro using the `#define` directive. For example, to obtain the area of a triangle, you can use the directive

```
#define area(base, height) (0.5 * base * height)
```

where `area` is the macro name, `base` and `height` are arguments, and the expression `(0.5*base*height)` is the macro definition.

Once you have defined a macro, you can use it anywhere in the program. For example, to calculate the `area` of a triangle whose `base` and `height` are 4.0 cm and 6.0 cm, you can write the statement

```
cout << "Area = " << area(4.0, 6.0);
```

Similarly, to find the average of four numbers (a, b, c, and d), you can use the following `#define` directive and statement:

```
#define avg(x, y) (x + y) / 2.0

avg4 = avg(avg(a, b), avg(c, d))
```

When the substitution is made, the statement will be as follows:

```
avg4 = ((a + b)/ 2.0 + (c + d) / 2.0) / 2.0
```

Although macros increase the speed of computation, they do have some drawbacks. Nesting macros can lead to hard-to-read code. Also, you cannot use pointers in macros.

Inline Functions

The *inline* function is preferable to a macro as it provides most of the features of macro but without its disadvantages. As in macro, the compiler will substitute the code for inline function wherever its name appears in the program. An inline function is a true function whereas a macro is not.

The definition of an inline function is similar to that of an ordinary function except that it also includes the keyword `inline` (placed before the function type). The main difference between an ordinary function and an inline function is that in the former the compiler does not substitute the code wherever it is called whereas in the latter it substitutes the code.

Program 6.10 illustrates inline functions. It computes the area of a triangle given its base and height.

Program 6.10

```
// Area of triangle using inline function
#include "pch.h"
#include <iostream>
using namespace std;
```

```
// inline function
inline double triangle_area(double base, double height)
{
    double area;
    area = 0.5 * base * height;
    return area;
}

void main()
{
    double b, h, a;
    b = 4; h = 6;
    // Compiler will substitute the inline function code
    a = triangle_area(b, h);
    cout << "Base = " << b << endl;
    cout << "Height = " << h << endl;
    cout << "Area = " << a << endl;
}
```

Output

```
Base = 4
Height = 6
Area = 12
```

An inline function executes faster as no function call is actually involved (remember functions require stack operations). There is however one main disadvantage: if the function is called frequently, your program gets longer.

6.9 Function Templates

You can use templates to write code that is independent of data types. Templates can be used to create generic functions (or classes). Using templates can also minimize code.

Program 6.11 illustrates this. It defines the template T for data type. The function maxi() takes two parameters (x and y) and returns the maximum - numerically or lexicographically (in the case of strings). In the place of data types, it uses template T for both function and parameter types. The code executes correctly for different data types – int, double and string.

Instead of writing three functions for the three pairs of parameter types, we used only one function using template.

Program 6.11

```
#include "pch.h"
#include <iostream>
#include <string>

using namespace std;

template <typename T>
T maxi(T x, T y)  //
{
    if (x < y)
        return y;
    else
        return x;
}
```

```
void main()
{
  int n1 = 15, n2 = 7;
  double f1 = 55.5, f2 = 99.9;
  string s1 = "alpha", s2 = "beta";
  cout << "\nMaximum of " << n1 << " and " << n2 << " = " << maxi(n1, n2);
  cout << "\nMaximum of " << f1 << " and " << f2 << " = " << maxi(f1, f2);
  cout << "\nMaximum of " << s1 << " and " << s2 << " = " << maxi(s1, s2);
  cout << endl;
}
```

Output

```
Maximum of 15 and 7 = 15
Maximum of 55.5 and 99.9 = 99.9
Maximum of alpha and beta = beta
```

You can define more than one template, e.g. T, U and V for different data types. Program 6.12 illustrates this. It uses T for data type int and U for data type double.

Program 6.12

```
#include "pch.h"
#include <iostream>
using namespace std;

template <typename T, typename U>
U maxi(T const& x, U const& y)   //
{
   if (x < y)
      return y;
   else
      return x;
}

void main()
{
   int n = 7;
   double d = 9.9;
   char c1 = 'B', c2 = 'Y';
   cout << "\nMaximum of " << n << " and " << d << " = " << maxi(n, d);
   cout << "\nMaximum of " << c1 << " and " << c2 << " = " << maxi(c1, c2);
}
```

Output

```
Maximum of 7 and 9.9 = 9.9
Maximum of B and Y = Y
```

Program 6.13 calculates the average of three integers and floating point numbers using a template.

Program 6.13

```
#include "pch.h"
#include <iostream>
using namespace std;

template <typename T>
T avg(T x, T y, T z)   //
{
     return (x+y+z)/3.0;
}
```

```
void main()
{
    int n1 = 5, n2 = 6, n3 = 7;
    float f1 = 9.9, f2 = 7.7, f3 = 8.8;
    cout << "\nAverage of integers: " << avg(n1, n2, n3);
    cout << "\nAverage of integers: " << avg(f1, f2, f3);
}
```

Output

```
Average of integers: 6
Average of integers: 8.8
```

6.10 Recursion

A function may call itself *recursively*. Such a function is called a **recursive** function. For example, to compute the factorial of a natural number, we can use

```
factorial(n) = 1                     for n = 0
             = n * factorial(n-1)    for n > 0
```

If n = 0, then `factorial(n)` = 1. This is called *anchor condition* for the function. In recursion, you must always have an anchor or else the function would not terminate. If n > 0, the function will call itself recursively.

Program 6.14 computes the factorial of n recursively.

Program 6.14
```
// Factorial(n) computation using recursion
#include "pch.h"
#include <iostream>
using namespace std;

void main()
{
    long factorial(int); // Function prototype
    long fact;
    int n;
    char ch;
    cout << "\nEnter number: ";
    cin >> n;
    fact = factorial(n);
    cout << "Factorial of " << n << " = " << fact << endl;
    cin.ignore();
    cin >> ch;
}

// Recursive factorial computation
long factorial(int n)
{
    if (n < 1) return 1;
    else return (n * factorial(n - 1));
}
```

Output

```
Enter number: 7
Factorial of 7 = 5040
```

86

The *fibonacci sequence*: 1, 1, 2, 3, 5, 8, 13, 21, ... where each number after the first two is the sum of the two preceding numbers can also be generated using recursion. A recursive function to generate the fibonacci sequence up to n is given in Program 6.15.

Program 6.15

```
// Fibonacci sequence using recursion
#include "pch.h"
#include <iostream>
using namespace std;

void main()
{
    int fib(int); // prototype
    int n;
    char ch;
    cout << "Enter n in fibonacci sequence: ";
    cin >> n;
    cout << "Next number in the sequence is: " << fib(n) << "\n";
}

int fib(int n)
{
    int fn;
    if (n == 0 || n == 1) return 1;
    fn = fib(n - 1) + fib(n - 2);
    return fn;
}
```

Output

```
Enter n in fibonacci sequence: 7
Next number in the sequence is: 21
```

Why do we need recursion? For example, we could have computed the factorial of a number without using recursion just as easily as in Program 6.16.

Program 6.16

```
// Factorial(n) computation without using recursion
#include "pch.h"
#include <iostream>
#include <string>
using namespace std;

void main()
{
    long factorial(int);
    long fact;
    int n;
    char ch;
    cout << "\nEnter number: ";
    cin >> n;
    fact = factorial(n);
    cout << "Factorial of n = " << fact << endl;
}

long factorial(int n)
{
    long fact = 1;
    while (n>1)
    {
```

```
        fact = fact * n;
        n--;
    }
    return fact;
}
```

Output

```
Enter number: 7
Factorial of n = 5040
```

Although many functions can be computed easily without using recursion, there are others that are lot easier to compute with recursion than without it, for example, the Hanoi Tower game problem shown below. This problem is difficult to solve without using recursion.

The Hanoi Tower Game Problem

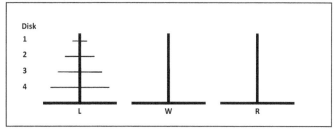

Given three pegs L, W and R (for Left, Work and Right) and a set of disks of varying sizes. Initially, all the disks are in peg L, arranged from the biggest at the bottom to the smallest at the top as shown below. The problem is to transfer the disks, one by one, from peg L to peg R using the work peg W given the rule that at any given instance, the set of disks in each peg must always be arranged from the biggest at the bottom to the smallest at the top.

This problem is best solved using recursion. A recursive function for the Hanoi tower game problem is given in Program 6.17.

The algorithm for moving n disks from L to R, using W is as follows:

1. If n = 1, move the single disk from L to R and stop
2. Move the top n-1 disks from L to W, using R as work
3. Move the remaining disk from L to R
4. Move the n-1 disks from W to R, using L as work

Program 6.17

```
#include "pch.h"
#include <iostream>
using namespace std;

void main(void)
{
    void transfer(int, char, char, char);
    int n;
    char ch;
    cout << "\nEnter number of disks: ";
    cin >> n;
```

88

```
        if (n > 0)
            transfer(n, 'L', 'R', 'W');
}

void transfer(int n, char from, char to, char work)
{
        if (n == 1)
        {
            cout << "\nMove disk 1 from peg " << from;
            cout << " to peg " << to;
        }

        else
        {
            // Move n-1 disks from source to work
            transfer(n-1, from, work, to);
            cout << "\nMove disk " << n << " from peg " << from;
            cout << " to peg " << to;
            // Move n-1 disks from work to destination
            transfer(n - 1, work, to, from);
        }
}
```

Sample output

```
Enter number of disks: 3

Move disk 1 from peg L to peg R
Move disk 2 from peg L to peg W
Move disk 1 from peg R to peg W
Move disk 3 from peg L to peg R
Move disk 1 from peg W to peg L
Move disk 2 from peg W to peg R
Move disk 1 from peg L to peg R
```

Exercise

1. Write functions to (a) right justify, (b) centre justify and (c) count the number of non-blank characters for a given string.

2. Write a function to remove embedded blanks in a string.

3. Write a function to replace all occurrences of character 'x' with 'X'.

4. Write a program using a template to calculate the area and circumference of a circle given its radius.

5. Write function to compute the number of tokens in a string.

6. Write a function to test if a given string is a palindrome. (A *palindrome* is a string where reading it forward and backward is the same, e.g. the strings madam and sagas and the numbers 12344321, 1234321 are palindromes whereas gorgeous and 12345 are not palindromes.)

7. Write a function to simulate a table-tennis game for doubles where one team has a 70 percent chance of winning each point.

Chapter 7

Arrays

Learning Outcomes:

After completing this chapter, the student will be able to

- *Declare one and two-dimensional arrays.*
- *Access array elements.*
- *Accessing array elements using pointers.*
- *Manipulate strings.*
- *Passing arrays to functions.*
- *Passing strings to functions.*

An array is a collection of elements of the *same* data type, all having the same common name. The elements occupy contiguous memory locations. An **index (or subscript)** is used to access the individual elements of the array. For example, if array `mark` stores student marks, we can access the i-th student's mark by writing `mark[i]`. By changing the value of `i`, we can access the mark of any student.

7.1 One-dimensional Arrays

A one-dimensional array declaration takes the form

```
data_type var_name[size];
```

The `data_type` specifies the base type of the array (`int`, `double`, `string`, etc.), which is also the type of each element in the array. The `size` defines the maximum number of elements the array can store. For example, we can declare an array of 20 characters using the statement

```
char ch[20];
```

The first character occupies position `[0]` and the last character occupies position `[19]`. The index ranges from 0 to 19 (not from 1 to 20).

Note: Array indexes always start from 0 and end with `size-1`.

Here are some examples of one-dimensional array declarations.

```
int x[20], y[50];
double price[10];
char letter[27];
string s[20];
```

The first statement declares arrays x and y of type `int`. Array x can store up to 20 integers and array y can store up to 50 integers. The second statement declares array `price` of type `double`. It can store up to 10 floating-point numbers. The third statement declares array `letter` of type `char`. It can store up to 26 characters. The last statement declares `s` of type string. It can store up to 20 strings.

Note:
1. C++ automatically terminates a string with a NULL character (the escape sequence \0).
2. You can declare arrays of the *same* type on the *same* line.
3. You can declare arrays and ordinary variables of the same type on the same line.

Array initialization

Arrays can be initialized when they are declared. Initialization of arrays take the form

```
type_specifier array_name[size] = {value_list};
```

Here are some examples of array declaration and initialization.

```
int id[7] = {1, 2, 3, 4, 5, 6, 7};
double x[5] = {5.5, 4.4, 3.3, 2,2, 1.1};
char vowel[6] = {'a', 'e', 'i', 'o', 'u', '\0'};
string s[4] = {"sally", "wong", "sam", "Mariam"};
```

Note:
1. Characters are enclosed with single quotes (') while strings are enclosed with double quotes (").
2. You need not specify the array size [ ] as C++ will automatically determine the size by looking at the number of elements assigned to it.

Character arrays can also be initialized more compactly as follows:

```
char array_name[size] = string;
```

For example, we can declare the array `vowel` compactly as follows:

```
char vowel[6] = "aeiou";
```

Passing one-dimensional array to function

C++ allows you to pass a pointer array to a function. For example, you can pass the address of array x to function `fn` as follows:

```
fn(double *x)      // pass pointer to function
fn(double x[5])    // pass sized array to function
fn(double x[])     // pass unsized array to function
```

The code below passes array address to a function using a pointer. It passes the address of x to the parameter `ptr`.

```
void main()
{
    double x[5];
    void fn(double *);  // function prototype
    fn (x) ;
}
```

```
void fn(double *ptr)
{

}
```

Accessing array elements

Program 7.1 declares and initializes array y. It uses a for loop with index i to access the elements of y. At each loop cycle, the value accessed is added to variable total which is finally displayed. The loop index i starts from 0 to 4 (not 1 to 5). We have declared the array size n using a #define statement. (Alternatively, you can use the statement int n = 4; to declare the array size.

Program 7.1

```
// Program to compute sum of all elements in array
#include "pch.h"
#include <iostream>
#include <string>
#define n 5   // n = 5
using namespace std;

void main()
{
      int i, total = 0, y[n] = { 9, 6, 20, 5, 12 };
      for (i = 0; i < n; i++)
            total = total + y[i];
      cout << "\nTotal = " << total;
      cin.ignore();
}
```

Output

```
Total = 52
```

Searching for a value in array

To search for an array item, you use a for loop and an if statement.

Program 7.2 finds the smallest element (value) in array balance. First, it assumes the smallest element is in balance[0] and assigns it to variable small. Then it compares small with the rest of the values in balance, one by one. If any element is smaller, it assigns it to small. This continues until the smallest element is placed in small. The program outputs 10.1, which is the smallest element in the array.

Program 7.2

```
//Program to find the smallest balance in array
#include "pch.h"
#include <iostream>
#include <string>
#define n 6
using namespace std;

void main()
{
      int i;
      double small;
      double balance[n] = { 100.50, 2575, 12.75, 20.4, 62.12, 10.15 };
      small = balance[0];
      for (i = 1; i < n; i++)
```

```
            if (small > balance[i]) small = balance[i];
        cout << "\nSmallest balance = " << small << endl;
}
```

Output

```
Smallest balance = 10.15
```

Swapping contents of variables

How do you swap the contents of two variables such as num1 and num2? Can we use the following statements?

```
        num1 = num2;
        num2 = num1;
```

The first statement assigns the value (contents) of num2 to num1. Now both num1 and num2 have the same value. The second statement would not produce the desired result.

To swap the contents of two variables, you need a third variable as follows:

```
        num3 = num1;
        num1 = num2;
        num2 = num3;
```

Sorting array elements

Many applications requites sorting, e.g. sorting numbers in ascending order of magnitude or sorting names in alphabetical order. There are many sorting algorithms available, some more efficient (in terms of processing time and/or memory) than others.

Program 7.3 illustrates sorting arrays using a simple algorithm (not necessarily efficient). It sorts a list of integers in array x [ ] in ascending order of magnitude.

Program 7.3

```
#include "pch.h"
#include <iostream>
#include <string>
#define n 7
using namespace std;

void main()
{
        int temp, i, j, x[] = { 22, 55, 99, 44, 33, 77, 11 };

        // Sort array
        for (i=0; i <n-1; i++)
        {
                for (j = i+1; j<n; j++)
                        if (x[i] > x[j])
                        {
                                temp = x[i];
                                x[i] = x[j];
                                x[j] = temp;
                        }
        }
        cout << "Sorted list: \n";
```

```
    for (i=0; i < n; i++)
        cout << x[i] << " ";
}
```

Output

```
Sorted List:
11 22 33 44 55 77 99
```

Let's explain how the nested for loops work. The outer loop index i is used for the first element in x and the inner loop index j is used for the second element in x. The search array is progressively reduced for each outer loop cycle. That is, for each i ($i = 1, 2, \ldots, n-1$), j only runs from i+1 to n. The if statement swaps the first element if it is greater than the second element.

7.2 Two-dimensional Arrays

Two-dimensional arrays have two subscripts (indexes). The first subscript is used for the row while the second subscript is used for the column. A two-dimensional array declaration takes the form

```
type array_name[size1][size2];
```

Here are some examples of two-dimensional array declarations.

```
double amount[5][7];
char ch[5][10];
int x[3][4];
```

The first statement declares amount as a floating-point array with 5 rows and 7 columns. The second statement declares ch as a character array with 5 rows and 10 columns. The last statement declares x as an integer array with 3 rows and 4 columns as shown below.

Subscripts for array x[3][4]

		Columns			
		0	1	2	3
Rows	0	[0][0]	0][0]	0][0]	0][0]
	1	[1][0]	[1][0]	[1][0]	[1][0]
	2	[2][0]	[2][0]	[2][0]	[2][0]

Strings can also be stored in a two-dimensional character array with the left index specifying the number of strings and the right index specifying the maximum length of each string. For example, to store the names of 4 persons, each with a maximum of 20 characters, we can declare as follows:

```
char name[4][20];
```

Alternatively we can declare the above using a string array as follows:

```
string name[4];   // string can be up to 255 characters
```

A two-dimensional array can be declared and initialized in one of the following ways:

```
int x[3][4] = {1,2,3,4,5,6,7,8,9,10,11,12};
int x[3][4] = {{1,2,3,4},{5,6,7,8},{9,10,11,12}}; // each row with {}
```

The result of these assignments would be as follows:

```
x[0][0] = 1      x[0][1] = 2       x[0][2] = 3      x[0][3] = 4
x[1][0] = 5      x[0][1] = 6       x[0][2] = 7      x[1][3] = 8
x[2][0] = 9      x[2][1] = 10      x[2][2] = 11     x[2][3] = 12
```

If the number of values assigned to an array is less the specified array size, C++ will assign zero to the missing positions. For example, for the statement

```
int x[3][4] = {1,2,3,4,5,6,7,8,9,10};
```

zero will be assigned to x[2][2] and x[2][3].

Similarly, for the statement

```
int x[3][4] = {{1,2,3},{5,6,7},{9,10,11}};
```

zero will be assigned to x[0][3], x[1][3] and x[2][3].

You can also fill an array with zeroes as follows:

```
int x[3][4] = {0};
```

You can also declare and initialize strings as follows:

```
char name[4][10] ={"Sophia", "Roland", Jane", "John"};
```

This will result in the following assignments:

```
name[0] = "Sophia"      name[1] = "Roland"
name[2] = "Jane"        name[3] = "John"
```

Here are some examples that illustrates two-dimensional arrays.

Program 7.4 calculates the average of all the values in array x by passing x and its dimensions, m and n, to the function get_average().

Program 7.4

```
#include "pch.h"
#include <iostream>
#define m 4
#define n 5
using namespace std;

void main()
{
    int x[m][n] = { { 4,5,6,2,12 },{ 10,25,33,22,11 }, { 21,32,43,54,65 },
                    { 3,2,1,5,61 } };
    double average;
    double get_average(int*, int, int); // function prototype
    average = get_average(*x, m, n);
    cout << "Average = " << average << endl;
}
```

95

```
double get_average(int *ptr, int x, int y)
{
    int i, total = 0;
    double average;

    for (i = 0; i < x * y; i++)
        total += *(ptr + i);
    average = (double)total / ((double)x * y);
    return average;
}
```

Output

```
Average = 20.85
```

Program 7.5 computes the square root of the sum of the squares of all positive values in array x. The loop index i is used to access the elements of y. At each loop cycle the value is added to total which is then printed.

Program 7.5

```
// Program to compute square root of the sum of all the
// squares of elements in array x
#include "pch.h"
#include <iostream>
#define m 4
#define n 5

using namespace std;

void main()
{
    int i, j;

    int x[m][n] = { { 4,5,6,2,12 },{ 10,25,33,22,11 },{ 21,32,43,54,65 },
                    { 3,2,1,5,61 } };
    double sum = 0, result = 0;
    for (i = 0; i < m; i++)
        for (j = 0; j < n; j++)
            if (x[i][j] > 0)
                sum = sum + pow(x[i][j], 2);
    result = sqrt(sum);
    cout << "Answer = " << result << endl;
}
```

Output

```
Answer = 129.842
```

Program 7.6 illustrates three nested for loops. It computes the product of matrix x and matrix y and stores the result in matrix z. Note for matrix multiplication, the number of columns of matrix x must be equal to the number of rows of matrix y.

Program 7.6

```
// Program that multiplies matrix x and matrix y and stores result in z
#include "pch.h"
#include <iostream>
#include <iomanip>
#define m 3
#define c 2
#define n 4
```

96

```
using namespace std;

void main()
{
    int i, j, k;
    int x[m][c] = { 1,2,3,4,5,6 };
    int y[c][n] = { 7,8,9,10,11,12,13,14 };
    int z[m][n];
    for (i = 0; i < m; i++)
        for (j = 0; j < n; j++)
        {
            z[i][j] = 0;
            for (k = 0; k < c; k++)
                z[i][j] += x[i][k] * y[k][j];
        }
    cout << "The matrix product is: \n";
    for (i = 0; i < m; i++)
    {
        cout << "\n";
        for (j = 0; j < n; j++)
            cout << setw(5) << z[i][j] << " ";
    }
}
```

Output

```
The matrix product is:

    29    32    35    38

    65    72    79    86

   101   112   123   134
```

Multidimensional Arrays

A array with more than two dimensions is called a **multi-dimensional** array. Its declaration is similar to the two dimensional array declaration. It takes the form

```
type name[size1][size2]...[sizeN];
```

For example,

```
int y[4][5][3];
```

declares a 3-dimensional array with four 4 by 5 by 3 elements.

7.3 Pointers to Arrays

An array name is really a pointer in disguise. When an array name is used without an index, it points to the *first* element (subscript [0]) of the array. For example, for the array declaration

```
int ary[5] = {2, 4, 6, 8, 10};
```

ary acts as a pointer to the first element ary[0].

When a string function is executed, only a pointer is passed to the string, not the actual string.

7.4 Pointer Arrays

We can also store pointers in an array. For example, you can declare a pointer array of size 20 of type int as follows:

```
int *arayptr[20];
```

To assign the address of an integer variable, say var, to the third element of the array, we can write

```
arayptr[2] = &var;
```

To access the value stored in var, we can write

```
*arayptr[2]
```

To pass a pointer array to a function, we simply call the function with the array name (without using any index). For example, to pass the array arayptr to function viewaray(), we can write the function as

```
viewaray(arayptr);
```

Program 7.7 shows how array pointers are passed to a function. First, the program declares and initializes the integer array variable var. Second, it assigns the address of each element (var[i]) to the corresponding pointer (arayptr[i]). Third, the pointer array arayptr is passed to viewaray(). The array parameter q[] receives the array passed. Fourth, the function displays the elements pointed to by q[] (i.e., the elements of array var). Finally, control passes to main() function.

Program 7.7

```
// passes pointer array to function
#include "pch.h"
#include <iostream>

using namespace std;

void main()
{
      int i, *arayptr[7], var[7] = { 0, 1, 2, 3, 4, 5, 6 };
      void viewaray(int *[]);        // prototype for viewaray
      for (i = 0; i < 7; i++)
            arayptr[i] = &var[i];    // assign address of var to arayptr[i]
      viewaray(arayptr);             // call function
}

// arayptr is passed q; q[i] points to var[i]
void viewaray(int *q[])
{
      int j;
      for (j = 0; j < 7; j++)
            cout << *q[j] << " ";    //display var[j]
      cout << endl;
}
```

Output

```
0 1 2 3 4 5 6
```

7.4 Sample Programs

Program 7.8 prints the `name`, `mark` and `grade` of n students.

Program 7.8

```
#include "pch.h"
#include <iostream>
#include <string>
using namespace std;
void main()
{
    string grade, name[] = { "Sally", "Wong", "Samson" };
    int i, n = 3, mark[] = { 77, 55, 48 };
    cout << "\nNo. Name        Mark\tGrade\n";
    for (i = 0; i < n; i++)
    {
        if (mark[i] < 50)
            grade = "Fail";
        else
            grade = "Pass";
        cout << i + 1 << "   " << name[i] << "\t" << mark[i] << "\t"
            << grade << endl;
    }
}
```

Output

```
No. Name      Mark    Grade
1   Sally     77      Pass
2   Wong      55      Pass
3   Samson    48      Fail
```

Program 7.9 calculates the salaries of n employees given their `basic` salary, `rate` and `hours` worked.

Program 7.9

```
#include "pch.h"
#include <iostream>
#include <string>
using namespace std;

void main()
{
    int i, n = 3;
    string name[] = { "Sally", "Wong", "Samson" };
    float basic[] = { 2345, 3200, 2570 };
    float rate[] = { 25, 30, 27 };
    int hours[] = { 12, 10, 15 };
    float pay;
    cout << "\nNo. Name\tBasic\tHours\tRate\tPay\n";
    for (i = 0; i < n; i++)
    {
        pay = basic[i] + hours[i] * rate[i];
        cout << i + 1 << "   " << name[i] << "\t" << basic[i] << "\t";
        cout << hours[i] << "\t" << rate[i] << "\t" << pay << endl;
    }
}
```

Output

No.	Name	Basic	Hours	Rate	Pay
1	Sally	2345	12	25	2645
2	Wong	3200	10	30	3500
3	Samson	2570	15	27	2975

Program 7.10 illustrates three ways of accessing array elements: using array subscript [i], using auto and using auto and address of. The size (x) function returns the length of array x.

Program 7.10

```
#include "pch.h"
#include <iostream>
using namespace std;

void main()
{
    int x[] = { 1, 2, 3, 4, 5, 6, 7 };
    cout << "Printing array elements in 3 ways:\n";
    for (int i = 0; i < size(x); i++)  // size(x) gives the length of array
        cout << x[i] << "  ";
    cout << endl;
    for (auto y : x)        // another way using auto
        cout << y << "  ";
    cout << endl;
    for (auto &y : x)       // another way using auto and address
        cout << y << "  ";
    cout << endl;
}
```

Output

```
Printing array elements in 3 ways:
1  2  3  4  5  6  7
1  2  3  4  5  6  7
1  2  3  4  5  6  7
```

Program 7.11 calculates the sum and average (avg) of the elements in array x.

Program 7.11

```
#include "pch.h"
#include <iostream>
#include <iomanip>
using namespace std;

void main()
{
    int x[] = { 111, 222, 333, 444, 555, 666, 777 };
    double sum = 0, avg;
    for (auto y : x)
        sum = sum + y;
    avg = sum / size(x);
    cout << "Sum = " << sum << endl;
    cout << "Average = " << setw(2) << avg << endl;
}
```

Output

```
Sum = 3108
Average = 444
```

Program 7.12 finds the position of a given number in x and displays the message Match found at

100

`position` ... or the message `No match found` if the number entered is not in the array.

Program 7.12

```
#include "pch.h"
#include <iostream>
using namespace std;

void main()
{
      int x[] = { 111, 222, 333, 444, 555, 666, 777 };
      int i, num, pos, n;
      bool flag = false;  // Boolean variable with initial value false
      n = size(x);
      cout << "Enter a number to match: ";
      cin >> num;
      for (i = 0; i < n; i++) // search for match
      {
            if (num == x[i])
            {
                  flag = true;
                  pos = i;
                  break;
            }
      }
      if (flag)
         cout << "Match found at position (starting from 0) = " << pos << endl;
      else
         cout << "No match found" << endl;
}
```

Sample runs:

```
Enter a number to match: 555
Match found at position (starting from 0) = 4

--

Enter a number to match: 245
No match found
```

Program 7.13 determines if a number is divisible by 7.

Program 7.13

```
#include "pch.h"
#include <iostream>
using namespace std;

void main()
{
      int x[] = { 11, 21, 37, 56, 94, 105, 123 };

      // find numbers that are divisible by 7
      for (auto num : x)
      {
            if (num % 7 == 0)  // check if divisible by 7
               cout << num << " is divisible by 7" << endl;
            else
                  cout << num << " is not divisible by 7" << endl;
      }
}
```

Output

```
11 is not divisible by 7
21 is divisible by 7
37 is not divisible by 7
56 is divisible by 7
94 is not divisible by 7
105 is divisible by 7
123 is not divisible by 7
```

Program 7.14 displays the internet code given the country name.

Program 7.14

```cpp
#include "pch.h"
#include <iostream>
#include <string>

using namespace std;

void main()
{
    int i, n;
    char ch;
    string country[] = { "vietnam", "india", "malaysia", "singapore",
                         "cambodia" };
    string code[] = { "vn", "in", "my", "sg", "kh" };
    string ctry;
    n = size(country);   // get no. of elements in country
    cout << "Enter country: ";
    cin >> ctry;
    // find country code
    for (i=0 ; i<n; i++)
    {
        if (ctry == country[i])
        {
            cout << "The country code for " << country[i] << " is: " <<
                    code[i] << endl;
            break;
        }
    }
}
```

Sample runs:

```
Enter country: malaysia
The country code  for Malaysia is my


--


Enter country: wonderland
The country code  for wonderland is not available
```

Program 7.15 lists the countries in array country using a pointer.

Program 7.15

```cpp
#include "pch.h"
#include <iostream>
#include <string>
using namespace std;
```

```
void main()
{
    int i, n;
    string *ptr, country[] = { "vietnam", "india", "malaysia",
                               "singapore", "cambodia" };
    n = size(country);
    ptr = country;  // pointer to country
    for (i=0 ; i<n; i++)
    {
        cout << *ptr << endl;  // get element pointed to by ptr
        ptr++;  // points to next element
    }
}
```

Output

```
vietnam
india
malaysia
singapore
cambodia
```

Program 7.16 calculates the sum and average (avg) of a set numbers using a pointer to function.

Program 7.16

```
#include "pch.h"
#include <iostream>
#include <string>
using namespace std;

void avg(int x[], int n)
{
    int i;
    double avg, sum = 0;
    int * ptr;
    ptr = x;  // point to array x
    for (i=0 ; i<n; i++)
    {
        sum = sum + *ptr;  // get the element pointed to by ptr
        ptr++;  // increment ptr to point to next item
    }
    avg = sum / n;
    cout << "Sum = " << sum << endl;
    cout << "Average = " << avg << endl;
}

void main()
{
    int i, n;
    int x[] = { 1, 2, 3, 4, 5, 6, 7 };
    n = size(x);
    avg(x, n);  // call function; pass x and n
}
```

Output

```
Sum = 28
Average = 4
```

Program 7.17 generates a set of 3-digit integer random numbers in array list. Then it sorts the numbers

103

in ascending order of magnitude. The random numbers are generated using the built-in functions `srand()` and `rand()`. The `time()` function is contained in the file header `<ctime>`.

Program 7.17

```cpp
// generate random numbers and sorts the numbers
#include "pch.h"
#include <iostream>
#include <string>
#include <ctime>  // need this for srand() function
#define n 8
using namespace std;

void main()
{
    int i, j, temp, list[n];
    srand(int(time(NULL)));  // time to seed random number generator
    cout << "\nGenerated list:\n";
    for (i = 0; i < n; i++)
    {
        list[i] = rand() % 1000; // generate 3-digit random number
        cout << list[i] << " ";
    }
    cout << "\n\nSorted list:\n";
    for (i = 0; i < n - 1; i++)
        for (j = i + 1; j < n; j++)
            if (list[i] > list[j])
            {
                temp = list[i];
                list[i] = list[j];
                list[j] = temp;
            }
    for (i = 0; i < n; i++)
        cout << list[i] << " ";
    cout << endl;
}
```

Sample run

```
Generated list:
131 940 187 780 481 772 248 817

Sorted list:
131 187 248 481 772 780 817 940
```

Program 7.18 generates n new lines using function `newline()`.

Program 7.18

```cpp
// generates n new lines
#include "pch.h"
#include <iostream>
using namespace std;

void main()
{
    void newline(int);
    int n = 5;
    newline(n);
}

void newline(int m)
{
```

104

```
    int i;
    for (i = 0; i < m; i++)
        cout << "\n";
}
```

Program 7.19 simulates a table-tennis game between two players, A and B, given that A has a 0.5 chance of winning each point. The `rand()` function returns a value between 0 and 1.

Program 7.19

```cpp
// simulates a table-tennis game between player A and B
// given A has the probability of 0.6 of winning each point
#include "pch.h"
#include <iostream>
#include <iomanip>
#include <ctime>

using namespace std;

void main()
{
    int count = 0, n = 20, a_point = 0, b_point = 0;
    double r, prob_a = 0.6;
    srand(int(time(NULL)));  // seed random number generator
    while (a_point <= n && b_point <= n)
    {
        count++;
        r = ((double)rand() / (RAND_MAX));
        if (r < prob_a)
            a_point += 1;
        else
            b_point += 1;
        cout << fixed;  // fix the output fields
        cout << setw(3) << r << "   ";
        if (count % 5 == 0)
            cout << endl;
    }

    if (a_point > n)
        cout << "\nA is the winner.";
    else
        cout << "\nB is the winner.";
    cout << endl;
}
```

Sample run

```
0.956999   0.138340   0.397870   0.145451   0.013184
0.511399   0.913266   0.916227   0.088046   0.112033
0.676748   0.806574   0.243904   0.056398   0.930204
0.819788   0.783959   0.995941   0.536302   0.417066
0.676717   0.468856   0.048555   0.932676   0.435499
0.886990   0.876858   0.702017   0.859279   0.937864
0.204901   0.933836   0.541063   0.684652   0.816492
0.857753   0.550249   0.144383   0.485183   0.178533
0.194830
A is the winner.
```

Program 7.20 uses two nested `for` loops to compute the total of all elements in array x with $r=4$ rows and $n=4$ columns.

Program 7.20

```
#include "pch.h"
#include <iostream>
#define r 4
#define c 4
#define n 4
using namespace std;

void main()
{
    int x[r][c] = { {1, 2, 3, 4 }, {5, 6, 7, 8 }, {9, 10, 11, 12},
                    {13, 14, 15, 16} };
    double sum = 0;
    for (int i = 0 ; i < n; i++)
        for (int j=0; j < n; j++)
            sum = sum + x[i][j];
    cout << "Sum = " << sum << endl;
}
```

Output

```
Sum = 136
```

Program 7.21 is equivalent the above program, but uses the auto feature to loop through all the elements of x.

Program 7.21

```
#include "pch.h"
#include <iostream>
#include <string>
#define r 4
#define c 4
using namespace std;

void main()
{
    int x[r][c] = { {1, 2, 3, 4 }, {5, 6, 7, 8 }, {9, 10, 11, 12},
                    {13, 14, 15, 16} };
    double sum = 0;
    // uses 2 nested loops
    for (auto &i : x)                // uses address of operator &
        for (auto &j : i)            // uses address of operator &
            sum = sum + j;
    cout << "Sum = " << sum << endl;
}
```

Output

```
Sum = 136
```

Program 7.22 uses the auto feature to loop through all the characters in string ss. It also tests for blanks to separate the words in the string.

Program 7.22

```
#include "pch.h"
#include <iostream>
#include <string>
using namespace std;
```

```
void main()
{
    string ss = "Quantum physics tells us that a particle can be here
                 and there at the same time";
    cout << ss << "\n\n";
    cout << "String tokens:" << endl;
    for (auto s : ss)
    {
        if (s == ' ')
        {
            cout << endl;
            continue;     // continue next loop cycle
        }

        else
            cout << s;
    }
    cout << endl;
}
```

Output

```
Quantum physics tells us that a particle can be here and there at the same time

String tokens:
Quantum
physics
tells
us
that
a
particle
can
be
here
and
there
at
the
same
time
```

Exercise

1. Given the string array country of size n=10. Read the names of the countries from the keyboard and store the names in the array. Then display the country names.

2. Given the integer array x of size n=10 with initial values. Calculate and print the average of all the numbers.

3. Given the two-dimensional integer array x[10][20] with initial values. How many of the elements in the array are (a) negative, (b) how many are positive; and (c) how many are zero.

4. Generate 100 unique integer random numbers in the range [1000, 9999] in array x[]. Sort the numbers in ascending order of magnitude. Give a number, search the array and display the message "Number found at position ..." if a match is found, or the message "Number not in array" if no match is found.

5. Given the floating-point array x[10][10] with initial values, find the sum of all the

   a) Diagonal elements
   b) Square of the numbers in the even rows (i.e., rows 1, 3, 5, 7, 9)
   c) Square root of the numbers in the odd columns (i.e., columns 0, 2, 4, 6, 8)

6. Given a string, find if a specified substring is in the string.

7. Write a program to count the number of vowels in a string.

8. Trace the output for the code below.

```cpp
#include <iostream>
#define n 7
void main()
{
    int i, x[n] = {11, 22, 33, 44, 55,66, 77};
    int *ptr, **ptr2;
    ptr = &x[0];
    cout << "\nPart 1: " << "\n";
    for (i = 0; i < n; i++)
    {
        cout << *ptr;
        ptr++;
    }
    cout << "\nPart 2: " << "\n";
    ptr = &x[6];
    ptr2 = &ptr;
    cout << **ptr2;
}
```

Chapter 8

Structures

Learning Outcomes:

After completing this chapter, the student will be able to

- *Explain structures.*
- *Declare and access structures.*
- *Declare nested structures.*
- *Manipulate structures.*
- *Pass structures to functions.*

Arrays store data of the same data type (`int, double, char, string`). You cannot store different data types in the same array. This is where structures come in - they allow you to store different data types in the same array. They are useful for storing *record-type* data. For example, you can store an employee's name (`string`), age (`int`), sex (`char`), and salary (`double`) in a structure.

8.1 Declaring Structures

A structure is a collection of related data items stored (and referenced) under one name. The structure elements need not be of the same data type. The elements can be of different data types.

To use a structure, you must first create a template for it. The elements in a structure are called structure elements or members of the structure. For example, you can declare a student record with fields `id` (identification number), `name, age` and `gender` as follows:

```
struct student
{
    string id;
    string name;
    int age;
    char gender;
}; // ends with a semicolon
```

The keyword `struct` tells the compiler `student` is a structure template. Note there is a semicolon after the closing bracket.

The compiler does not allocate memory for structure templates until it is declared. You can declare structure variables in any of the following ways:

First method

```
struct student
{
```

```
       string id;
       string name;
       int age;
       char gender;
   } stud_1, stud_2;
```

Second method

```
   struct student
   {
       string id;
       string name;
       int age;
       char gender;
   };

   struct student stud_1, stud_2;
```

Both methods declare two structure variables `stud_1` and `stud_2`. Each structure variable has 4 elements – 3 character variables and an integer variable. In the first method, the structure variables are declared immediately after the closing bracket whereas in the second method they are declared as type `student`.

8.2 Accessing Structures

To access structure elements, we can use the statements

```
   stud_1.id = "B12";
   stud_1.name = "Mariam";
   stud_1.age = 25;
   stud_1.gender = 'F';
```

This will assign B2 to element id, `Mariam` to `name`, `25` to `age` and F to `gender` in structure variable `stud_1`. The dot operator qualifies that the variables are elements of the structure variable.

8.3 Array of Structures

You can also create array of structures. For example, to store the details of 50 students, you can declare in one of following ways:

| ```
struct student
{
    string id;
    string name;
    int age;
    char gender;
} stud[50];
``` | ```
struct student
{
    string id;
    string name;
    int age;
    char gender;
};
student stud[50];
``` |
|---|---|

Each declares an array `stud[]` of 50 structures of type `student`.

With this declaration, we can use a subscript to reference the individual elements of the structure. For example, to print the name of the seventh student, we can use the statement

```
cout << stud[6].name;
```

To initialize id, name, and gender to blank and age 0 for all students, we can use a for loop as follows:

```
for (i = 0; i<50; i++)
{
    stud[i].id = " ";
    stud[i].name = " ";
    stud[i].gender = '';
    stud[i].age = 0;
}
```

8.4 Passing Structures to Functions

Individual structure elements can be passed to a function. For example, to modify the name of the seventh student, we can use the function call

```
modify(stud[6].name);
```

This passes the structure element name of the seventh student to modify function. Only a copy of name is passed to the function. Any changes made to name in the called function will not affect the name in the calling function as they have different scopes. This is *calling by value*.

An entire structure can also be passed to a function. You can do this by passing the structure as an argument or by passing the address of the structure. For example, to modify the details of the seventh element in the structure, we can write

```
modify(stud[6]);
modify(&stud[6]);
```

The first statement passes a copy of the structure to the function while the second passes the address of the structure. In the first statement, any changes made to the structure in the called function will not affect the structure in the calling function. This is *calling by value*. In the second statement, any changes made to the structure in the called function will also affect the structure in the calling function because they share the same memory area. This is *calling by reference*.

Program 8.1 illustrates passing structures to functions. It declares structure vegetable with two fields, name and price. As this is global declaration, it is available to all functions in the program.

The main() function declares structure variables veg1 and veg2 of type vegetable, then calls function addname() to get name and price of the first vegetable. The function addname() gets these values and stores them in vege which is then assigned to veg1 in main().

Similarly, veg2 is assigned the name and price of the second vegetable. The main() then calls the function list_func() to print the information contained in structures veg1 and veg2 by passing them as arguments to function.

Program 8.1

```
// passing structures to functions
```

111

```cpp
#include "pch.h"
#include <iostream>
#include <string>
using namespace std;

struct vegetable // Ddine structure
{
     string name;
     float price;
} veg1, veg2;  // declare 2 variables of type structure (vegetable)

void main()
{
     char ch;
     vegetable addname();        // declare function prototype
     void list_vege(vegetable);   // declare function prototype
     veg1 = addname();
     veg2 = addname();
     cout << "\nVegetables for sale:\n";
     list_vege(veg1);  // pass structure veg1 to function
     list_vege(veg2);
}

vegetable addname()  // structure function
{
     vegetable vege;    // declare vege structure
     cout << "\nEnter vegetable name: ";
     cin >> vege.name;
     cout << "Enter price (per 100gm): $";
     cin >> vege.price;
     return(vege);
}

void list_vege(vegetable list)
{
     cout << "\nVegetable name: $" << list.name;
     cout << "\nVegetable price: $" << list.price;
}
```

Sample run

```
Enter vegetable name: cabbage
Enter price (per 100gm): $2.75

Enter vegetable name: brinjal
Enter price (per 100gm): $3.20

Vegetables for sale:
cabbage  Price = $2.75
broccoli Price = $3.2
```

8.5 Nested Structures

Structures can be nested, meaning, one structure may contain another structure. To illustrate, let's consider
the below two structures:

```cpp
struct student   // student structure
{
    string id;
```

```
   string name;
   char gender;
   int age;
};

struct detail  // detail structure
{
   string id;
   string name;
   char gender;
   int age;
   string course;
} stud_detaill;

stud_id = stud_detaill.id;
```

We can simplify the above code by writing

```
struct student
{
   string id;
   string name;
   char gender;
   int age;
};

struct detail
{
   student stud_1;        // use student structure
   string course;
} stud_detaill;

stud_id = stud_detaill.stud_1.id;
```

The stud_detail has two elements: stud_1 and course. The last statement assigns stud_1 id in stud_detaill to the variable stud_id.

Note that there are two dots in the statement. The first dot tells that the variable following it belong to structure stud_detaill while the second dot tells that the variable following it belongs to structure stud_1.

Program 8.2 illustrates nested structures. It declares structure position whose elements are structures: north and south (of type country). The program prints structure elements name and areacode contained in structures north and south.

Program 8.2

```
// illustrates structures
#include "pch.h"
#include <iostream>
#include <string>
using namespace std;

struct country     // declare structure type
{
     string ctry;
     string code;
};

void main()
{
```

```
country c1 = { "india", "in" };
country c2 = { "vietnam", "vn"};
cout << "Country\t\tCode" << endl;
cout << c1.ctry << "\t\t" << c1.code << endl;
cout << c2.ctry << "\t\t" << c2.code << endl;
}
```

Output

```
Country        Code
india          in
vietnam        vn
```

8.6 Linked Lists

Structures can be used as nodes in a linked list. A linked consists of a set of connected structures (nodes) using pointers. The basic idea is each node in a linked list contains a pointer to the next node. The pointer in the last node does not point to anything and so it is given the value NULL.

Linked lists can be used to create complex data structures such as linear lists (see Figure 6.2), circular lists (see Figure 6.3) and trees (see Figure 6.4).

Figure 6.2: A linear linked list

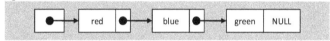

Figure 6.3: A circular linked list

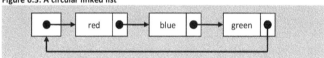

Figure 6.4: A tree

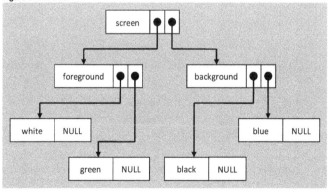

Here is an example of a linked list.

```
struct list
{
    string color ;
    list *next; // pointer to next node
}
```

The code declares a structure `list`. It consists of two members: string array `color` and pointer `next` to the next node.

To access structure elements using pointers, we use the combined operator `->` (consisting of minus and greater-than signs, treated as a single operator).

Program 8.3 illustrates pointer to structures. It declares structure `var` and pointer `ptr`. Then it assigns the address of `var` to `ptr`. The elements of `var` are assigned values and displayed.

Program 8.3

```
// pointer to structure
#include "pch.h"
#include <iostream>
using namespace std;

void main()
{
    struct temp
    {
        int num;
        char ch;
    };

    temp var;           // declare structure variable
    temp *ptr;          // declare pointer to structure
    ptr = &var;         // assign address of struct to ptr
    ptr->num = 501;     // access structure members
    ptr->ch = 'x';
    cout << "\n\nptr->num = " << ptr->num;
    cout << "\nptr->ch = " << ptr->ch << endl;
}
```

Output

```
ptr->num = 501
ptr->ch = x
```

The `new` operator can be used to create structures dynamically. The compiler will allocate just enough memory to accommodate the structures. For example, to create a structure of type `temp`, you can use the `new` operator as follows:

```
    temp ptr = new temp;
```

The statement assigns the address of structure `temp` to pointer `ptr`.

Program 8.4 illustrates the use of `new` operator in a linked list. It provides a menu of three items: add flight (to a linked list), list all flight information and exit. It uses three pointers to structures: `firstptr`, `thisptr` and `newptr` and the `new` operator. (You will need three pointers for manipulating linked lists: one to the first structure, one to the current structure and one to the previous structure.) Note the program initially assigns the NULL value (after casting it to structure `flight`) to pointer `firstptr`.

Program 8.4

```cpp
#include "pch.h"
#include <iostream>
#define TRUE 1
#define FALSE 0
using namespace std;

void new_flight(); // prototype
void list_flight();

struct flight // declaring structure
{
    char number[7];
    double fare;
    struct flight *ptrnext; // declare pointer to structure
};

// declare 3 pointers
flight *firstptr, *thisptr, *newptr;

void main()
{
    char ch;
    int choice = TRUE;
    firstptr = NULL; // initialize pointer to null

    while (choice == TRUE)
    {
        // Menu
        cout << "\nE - Enter flight number";
        cout << "\nL - List all flights";
        cout << "\nX - Exit\n";
        cout << "\nEnter choice: ";
        cin >> ch;
        ch = toupper(ch); // convert to uppercase

        switch (ch)
        {
            case 'E': new_flight(); break;
            case 'L': list_flight(); break;
            case 'X': choice = FALSE; break;
            default: cout << "\nOnly one of the above";
        }
    }
}

// enter new flight information
void new_flight()
{
    // create new structure of type flight and
    // make newptr point to this structure
    newptr = new flight;
    if (firstptr == NULL) // check if pointer is NULL
        firstptr = thisptr = newptr; //link one structure to another
    else
    {
        thisptr = firstptr;
        while (thisptr->ptrnext != NULL)
        thisptr = thisptr->ptrnext;
        thisptr->ptrnext = newptr; // link to new structure
        thisptr = newptr;
    }
```

116

```
        cout << "\nEnter flight number: ";
        cin >> thisptr->number;
        cout << "Enter fare: ";
        cin >> thisptr->fare;
        thisptr->ptrnext = NULL; // last structure points to NULL
}

// list flight information
void list_flight()
{
        if (firstptr == NULL) cout << "\nEmpty list";
        thisptr = firstptr;
        do // list all flight information
        {
                cout << "\n\nFlight number: " << thisptr->number;
                cout << "\nFare : $" << thisptr->fare << endl;
                thisptr = thisptr->ptrnext;
        } while (thisptr != NULL);  // continue until no more flights
}
```

Sample run

```
E - Enter flight number
L - List all flights
X - Exit
Enter choice: L
Flight number: MH55
Fare: 555.00

E - Enter flight number
L - List all flights
X - Exit

Enter choice: E
Flight number: SQ77
Fare: 777.00

E - Enter flight number
L - List all flights
X - Exit

Enter choice: L
Filght number: MH55
Fare: $555.00
Flight number: SQ77
Fare : $777.00

E - Enter flight number
L - List all flights
X - Exit

Enter choice: X
```

8.7 Sample Programs

Program 8.5 declares structure country, then creates a structure array c[] and displays the its contents.

Program 8.5

```
// illustrates array of structures
```

```
#include "pch.h"
#include <iostream>
#include <string>
using namespace std;

struct country    // declare structure
{
     string ctry;
     string code;
} ;

void main()
{
     country c[] = { { "india", "in" }, { "vietnam", "vn"},
                     {"china", "cn"}, {"myanmar", "mm"} };
     cout << "Country\t\tCode" << endl;
     for (auto cc: c)
        cout << cc.ctry << "\t\t" << cc.code << endl;
}
```

Output

```
Country      Code
india        in
vietnam      vn
china        cn
myanmar      mm
```

Program 8.6 declares structure book consisting of fields title, author and cost. It receives book details from the console, then displays the information in two different formats.

Program 8.6

```
// illustrates array of structures
#include "pch.h"
#include <iostream>
#include <string>
#define n 2
using namespace std;

struct book
{
     string title;
     string author;
     float price;
};

void main()
{
     int i;
     string sprice;
     book bk[n];
     for (i = 0; i < n; i++)
     {
          cout << "\nEnter book title: ";
          getline(cin, bk[i].title, '\n'); // reading multiple words
          cout << "Enter author: ";
          getline(cin, bk[i].author, '\n');
          cout << "Enter price: ";
          getline(cin, sprice, '\n');
          bk[i].price = atof(sprice.c_str());
     }
```

118

```
      cout << "\n\nNo. Author\t\tTitle\t\t\t\tPrice\n";
      for (i = 0; i < n; i++)
      {
            cout << i + 1 << "   " << bk[i].author << "\t\t" <<
                  bk[i].title << "\t\t";
            cout << setprecision(5) << bk[i].price << endl;
      }
}
```

```
Enter book title: Software Engineering
Enter author: Sommerville
Enter price: 79.90

Enter book title: Learn Python Ver 3
Enter author: Sellappan
Enter price: 49.70
```

No.	Author	Title	Price
1	Sommerville	Software Engineering	79.9
2	Sellappan	Learn Python Ver 3	49.7

Program 8.7 declares structure `fraction` consisting of `numerator` and `denominator`, then creates an array of `fraction` and displays the fractions using a loop.

Program 8.7

```
// displays increasing fractal number
#include "pch.h"
#include <iostream>
using namespace std;

struct fraction
{
      int numerator;
      int denominator;
};

void main()
{
      fraction frac[9];

      for (int i = 0; i < 9; ++i)
      {
            frac[i].numerator = i + 1;
            frac[i].denominator = 10; // set the denominator to 10
            cout << frac[i].numerator << "/";
            cout << frac[i].denominator << "\n";
      }
}
```

Output

```
1/10
2/10
3/10
4/10
5/10
6/10
7/10
8/10
9/10
```

Program 8.8 declares structure `item` of type `itemType`. Then it uses a pointer to call the `increase` function to increase the price by 10 %. Then it displays the before and after prices.

Program 8.8

```cpp
// uses pointer to structure to increase item price
#include "pch.h"
#include <iostream>
#include <string>
using namespace std;

struct itemType
{
    int itemNum;
    string itemName;
    double price;
};

void increase(itemType *pointer)
{
    (*pointer).price = (*pointer).price * 1.1;
}

void main()
{
    itemType item = { 1023, "Pencil", 2.50 };
    cout << "\nBefore price increase: \n";
    cout << "\nItem number:\t " << item.itemNum;
    cout << "\nItem name: \t " << item.itemName;
    cout << "\nItem price: \t $" << item.price << endl;

    increase(&item);   // increase price
    cout << "\nAfter price increase: \n";
    cout << "\nItem number:\t " << item.itemNum;
    cout << "\nItem name: \t " << item.itemName;
    cout << "\nItem price: \t $" << item.price;
    cout << endl;
}
```

Output

```
Before price increase:

Item number:    1023
Item name:      Pencil
Item price:     $2.5

After price increase:

Item number:    1023
Item name:      Pencil
Item price:     $2.75
```

Program 8.9 updates customer accounts. It has two structure variables, `date` and `record`. It reads, processes and prints each customer's details.

Program 8.9

```cpp
// update customer accounts
#include "pch.h"
#include <iostream>
#include <string>
using namespace std;
```

120

```cpp
typedef struct
{
      int month;
      int day;
      int year;
} date;

typedef struct
{
      string name;
      int acct_no;
      float bal;
      float payment;
      date lastpaymt;
} record;

// write current customer information
void writeoutput(record customer)
{
      cout << "\nName: " << customer.name;
      cout << "\t\t\t\t\tAccount no. : " << customer.acct_no;
      cout << "\nCurrent payment: " << customer.payment;
}

record readinput(int i)
{
      record customer; // read input data for a customer
      cout << "\nCustomer No." << i + 1;
      cout << "\nName: ";
      cin >> customer.name;
      cout << "\nAccount no.: ";
      cin >> customer.acct_no;
      cout << "\nCurrent payment: ";
      cin >> customer.payment;
      cout << "\nPayment date (mm dd yyyy): ";
      cin >> customer.lastpaymt.month;
      cin >> customer.lastpaymt.day;
      cin >> customer.lastpaymt.year;
      return(customer);
}

// read customer accounts, process and print
void main()
{
      int i, n;
      record customer[100];
      record readinput(int i);
      cout << "\t\tCUSTOMER BILLING SYSTEM\n\n";
      cout << "How many customers? ";
      cin >> n;
      for (i = 0; i < n; ++i)
      {
            customer[i] = readinput(i);
            writeoutput(customer[i]);
      }
}
```

Sample run

```
CUSTOMER BILLING SYSTEM
```

```
How many customers? 2

Customer No.1
Name: Nicole Newman
Account no.: 30221
Current payment: 20.00
Payment date (mm/dd/yyyy): 02 26 93
Customer No.2
Name: Jason Chan
Account no.: 41176
Current payment: 3000
Payment date (mm/dd/yyyy): 08 08 93

Name: Nicole Newman          Account no: 30221
Current payment: 20

Name: Jason Chan             Account no: 41176
Current payment: 3000
```

Exercise

1. Write a program using structure comprising club member name, area code and telephone number. Enter values for each member and display theeit information by area code.

2. Initialize a structure that has members' names and birthdays. Display the names of those who were born on a given date.

3. Declare a nested structure as follows:

    Student ID
    Name made up of first name, middle name, last name
    Date of birth made up of day, month and year
    An array of five courses
    An array of five marks

4. Given the below structure:

    ```
    struct account
    {
        string acc_no;
        string acc_type;
        string name;
        double balance;
    };
    ```

    Create an array of accounts and assign values for the members of each structure and display their information with suitable headings.

Chapter 9

Text Files

Learning Outcomes:

After completing this chapter, you will be able to

- *Explain file streams.*
- *Perform input/output using file streams.*
- *Read data from text files.*
- *Write data to text files.*

Data stored in the computer's RAM are volatile – they are lost when you switch off your computer. To store data permanently, you need to store the data on secondary storage devices like the hard disk or thumb drive.

Storage of data n secondary storage devices take the form of files e.g., database or text files. Here, we will only discuss text files.

Text files can be used for both input and output. You can store your input data in a text file and later make your program read the data. Similarly, you can send your output (results) to a text file for later use.

9.1 File Streams

File input/output in C++ uses two file streams: `ifstream` and `ofstream`. The `ifstream` is used for reading input data from a text file. The `ofstream` is used for sending output to a text file. To use these file streams, you can include the below directive.

```
#include <fstream>
```

With this directive, you can declare input/output file streams as follows:

```
ifstream infile;  // infile is an ifstream object
ofstream ofile;   // ofile is an ofstream object
```

Using these input/output streams, you can perform input/output on text files.

Before you can use text files, you need to open them as follows (your file directory path may be different):

```
// note double backslash \\ in file path
infile.open("C:\\Users\\Sellappan\\Desktop\\test.txt");
ofile.open("C:\\Users\\Sellappan\\Desktop\\results.txt");
```

Note that the file path has the double backslash escape sequence (\\). This is necessary; otherwise the compiler would interpret the escape sequence \U as Unicode character which would result in error.

Opening input text file (**test.txt**) allows you to read data from it. Similarly, opening output file (**results.txt**) allows you to send (write) data to it.

Reading input

To read data from a text file, first check if the file exists!   You can do this as follows:

```
if (!infile)   // check if the file exists
{
    cout << "Cannot open file!\n";
    exit(1);   // abnormal termination
}
```

To read a line from the file, you can use the function

```
getline(infile, line) //read a line of text and store it in variable line
```

To read multiple lines of input, you can use a loop such as

```
// check if there is more input; if not, terminate the loop
while (getline(infile, line))
{
    cout << line << endl;   // print the line
}
```

Writing output

Writing output to a text file works in a similar way. If the output file (results.txt) exists, it will overwrite it; if it doesn't exist, it will create one.

To write output to a text file you can use the statement

```
ofile << "This is my output" << endl;
```

After using the input/output files, you must remember to close them as follows:

```
infile.close();   // close input file

ofile.close();    // close output file
```

9.2 Reading Input from Text Files

You can read data from a text file using the following steps:

1. Create a text file for input using the Notepad program and save it with .txt extension.

2. Include the fstream directive as follows:

    ```
    #include <fstream>
    ```

3. Declare an input file stream object (infile) as follows:

    ```
    ifstream infile;   // infile is a ifstream object
    ```

4. Open the input file using the statement

```
infile.open("C:\\Users\\Sellappan\\Desktop\\test.txt");
```

5. Read the first line of input and store it in the variable line as follows:

```
getline(infile, line)
```

6. To read multiple lines of input use the loop as follows:

```
while (getline(infile, line))
{
     cout << line << endl;  // print the line
}
```

Program 9.1 illustrates reading data from a text file (test.txt). If the file doesn't exist, it will terminate via exit(1). Otherwise, it will read data until there is no more data in the file (step 6).

Program 9.1

```
#include "pch.h"
#include <iostream>
#include <fstream>
#include <string>

using namespace std;

void main()
{
     string line;
     ifstream infile;  // declare object for ifstream

     infile.open("C:\\Users\\Sellappan\\Desktop\\mark.txt");

     if (!infile)
     {
          cout << "Cannot open file!\n";
          exit(1); // exit program
     }

     while (getline(infile, line))
     {
          cout << line << endl;
     }

     infile.close();  // close file stream
}
```

Input file

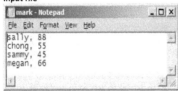

125

Output

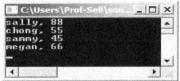

Program 9.2 reads a line of text, then separates the items - name and mark – delimited (separated) by comma. The variable pos finds the position of comma (,) in line. Then function substr(0, pos) extracts the name (characters from 0 to pos) and the function substr(pos+1) extracts the rest of the characters (from pos to end of line) for smark (string type). The function atoi (smark.c_str()) converts smark to integer mark.

Program 9.2

```
#include "pch.h"
#include <iostream>
#include <fstream>
#include <string>
using namespace std;

void main()
{
    string name, smark, grade, line;
    int mark, pos;
    ifstream infile;
    infile.open("C:\\Users\\Prof-Sell\\Desktop\\mark.txt");
    if (!infile)
    {
        cout << "Cannot open file!\n";
        exit(1);
    }
    cout << "Name\tMark\tGrade" << endl;

    while (getline(infile, line))
    {
        pos = line.find(','); // find the postion of , in line
        name = line.substr(0, pos);  // extract the name
        smark = line.substr(pos + 1); // extract the mark
        mark = atoi(smark.c_str());  // convert smark to integer
        if (mark < 50)
            grade = "Fail";
        else
            grade = "Pass";
        cout << name << "\t" << mark << "\t" << grade << endl;
    }
    infile.close();
}
```

Output

126

What if you have multiple items (fields) in each line of input, for example, name, basic pay, overtime hours worked and rate? You can use the same approach to extract the fields one by one. Program 9.3 illustrates this.

Program 9.3

```
#include "pch.h"
#include <iostream>
#include <fstream>
#include <string>
#include <iomanip>
using namespace std;

void main()
{
    string name, sbasic, shours, srate, line;
    float basic, rate, pay;
    int hours, pos;
    ifstream infile;
    infile.open("C:\\Users\\Prof-Sell\\Desktop\\salary.txt");
    if (!infile)
    {
        cout << "Cannot open file!\n";
        exit(1);
    }
    cout << "Name    Basic    Hours    Rate    Pay($)" << endl;
    while (getline(infile, line))
    {
        pos = line.find(',');
        name = line.substr(0, pos);
        line = line.substr(pos + 1); // work on truncated string
        pos = line.find(',');
        sbasic = line.substr(0, pos);
        basic = atof(sbasic.c_str());   // convert to float
        line = line.substr(pos + 1);
        pos = line.find(',');
        shours = line.substr(0, pos);
        hours = atoi(shours.c_str());
        line = line.substr(pos + 1);
        pos = line.find(',');
        srate = line.substr(0, pos);
        rate = atof(srate.c_str());   // convert to float
        pay = basic + hours * rate;
        cout << fixed;
        cout << name << "    " << sbasic << "    " << shours << "    " <<
                srate << "    " << setprecision(2) << pay << endl;
    }
    infile.close();
}
```

Input file

```
sally, 2200.00, 20, 25.00
chong, 3200.00, 15, 35.00
sammy, 3000.00, 12, 45.00
megan, 2900.00, 25, 20.00
```

127

Output file

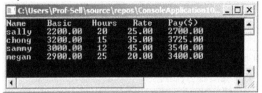

If there are several fields in a line (separated by comma), a better approach would be to use a loop to separate the items. Program 9.4 illustrates this. There are four input fields in a `line` – `name`, `basic`, `hours` and `rate`. The program uses array `vec[4]` to hold the fields of the `line`.

Program 9.4

```
#include "pch.h"
#include <iostream>
#include <fstream>
#include <string>
using namespace std;

void main()
{
    string line, name, vec[4];
    float basic, rate, pay;
    int i, hours, pos;
    ifstream infile;
    //note double \\ escape character
    infile.open("C:\\Users\\Prof-Sell\\Desktop\\salary.txt");

    if (!infile)
    {
        cout << "Cannot open file!\n";
        exit(1);
    }

    cout << "Name     Basic    Hours    Rate    Pay($)" << endl;
    while (getline(infile, line))
    {
        for (i = 0; i < 4; i++)
        {
            pos = line.find(',');
            vec[i] = line.substr(0, pos); // store item by item
            line = line.substr(pos + 1);  // work on truncated line
        }
        name = vec[0];  // store name
        basic = atof(vec[1].c_str());  // convert string basic to float
        hours = atoi(vec[2].c_str());  // convert string hours to int
        rate = atof(vec[3].c_str());
        pay = basic + hours * rate;
        cout << fixed;  // set output to fixed width
        cout << setprecision(2); // 2 decimal places
        cout << name << "  " << basic << "    " << hours << "     " <<
                rate << "    " << pay << endl;
    }
    infile.close();
}
```

128

9.3 Writing Output to Text Files

Sending output to text files work in a similar way.

1. Include the fstream directive as follows:

    ```
    #include <fstream>
    ```

2. Declare an output file stream object (ofile) as follows:

    ```
    ofstream ofile;  // ofile is a ofstream object
    ```

    Open the output file using the statement

    ```
    ofile.open("C:\\Users\\Sellappan\\Desktop\\results.txt");
    ```

Program 9.5 illustrates sending/writing output to a text file. It writes Hello World! to the text file out.txt. The output file stream is ofstream and the stream object is ofile.

Program 9.5

```cpp
#include "pch.h"
#include <iostream>
#include <fstream>
#include <string>
using namespace std;

void main()
{
    string s = "Hello world!";
    ofstream ofile;  // declare ofstream object
    ofile.open("C:\\Users\\Prof-Sell\\Desktop\\out.txt");
    ofile << s << endl;  // send output to file
    ofile.close();  // close file stream
}
```

Output file

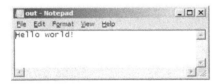

Program 9.6 is another example. It computes students' grades given their names and marks.

Program 9.6

```cpp
// send output to file
#include "pch.h"
#include <iostream>
#include <fstream>
#include <string>
using namespace std;

void main()
{
```

129

```
string grade, name[] = { "sally", "chong", "sammy", "megan" };
int i, mark[] = { 88, 55, 45, 66 };
ofstream ofile;
ofile.open("C:\\Users\\Prof-Sell\\Desktop\\grade.txt");

ofile << "Name\tMark\tGrade" << endl;

for (i = 0; i < 4; i++)
{
    if (mark[i] < 50)
        grade = "Fail";
    else
        grade = "Pass";
    ofile << name[i] << "\t" << mark[i] << "\t" << grade << endl;
}
ofile.close();
}
```

Output file

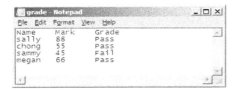

9.4 Reading from and Writing to Text Files

You can use several input/output files as your application requires by declaring an input/output stream object for each file. Program 9.7 illustrates reading input from one text file and writing output to another file.

Program 9.7
```
// reading input from text file - salary
// and sending output to text file - payroll
#include "pch.h"
#include <iostream>
#include <fstream>
#include <string>
#include <iomanip>
using namespace std;

void main()
{
    string line, name, vec[4];  // vec[] stores the input fields
    float basic, rate, pay;
    int i, hours, pos;
    ifstream infile;
    ofstream ofile;
    // input file
    infile.open("C:\\Users\\Prof-Sell\\Desktop\\salary.txt");
    // output file
    ofile.open("C:\\Users\\Prof-Sell\\Desktop\\payroll.txt");

    if (!infile)  // check if file exists
    {
        cout << "Cannot open file!\n";
```
130

```
            exit(1);
    }

    ofile << "Name     Basic    Hours    Rate    Pay($)" << endl;
    while (getline(infile, line)) // read input line
    {
            for (i = 0; i < 4; i++)
            {
                    pos = line.find(',');
                    vec[i] = line.substr(0, pos);
                    line = line.substr(pos + 1);
            }

            // split the fields
            name = vec[0];
            basic = atof(vec[1].c_str());   // convert to float
            hours = atoi(vec[2].c_str());   // convert to int
            rate = atof(vec[3].c_str());
            pay = basic + hours * rate;
            ofile << fixed;    // to fixed width
            ofile << setprecision(2); // to 2 decimal places
            ofile << name << "    " << basic << "     " << hours << "     " <<
                    rate << "     " << pay << endl;
    }
    infile.close();   // close infile stream
    ofile.close();
}
```

Input file

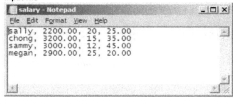

Output file

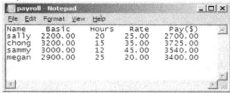

Exercise

1. Create an input text file (menu.txt) with fields name and price for n = 10 menu items. Write a program to read and print the data line by line.

2. Using the text file in question 1, write a program to read the data, extract the fields, store them in variables name and price, and print the fields as follows:

```
No.  Menu          Price
1       xxx         xxx.xx
2       xxx         xxx.xx
...
```

3. Write a program to generate 50 integer random numbers between 500 and 900 and write the numbers to a text file (random.txt).

4. Write a program to generate even numbers 2, 4, 6, ..., 100 and write the numbers to a text file (even.txt) – 10 numbers to a line.

5. Create a text file (author.txt) with fields author, title, publisher, price and year for n = 7 books. Write a program to read the fields and write them to a text file (book.txt) that resembles as follows:

```
No.  Author        Title            Price      Year
1       xxx         xxx              xxx.xx     xxxx
2       xxx         xxx              xxx.xx     xxxx
...
```

Chapter 10

Classes

Learning Outcomes:

After completing this chapter, the student will be able to

- *Explain class and its data and function members.*
- *Explain class and instance variables.*
- *Define and instantiate classes.*
- *Explain function and operator overloading.*
- *Explain constructors and destructors.*
- *Create arrays of objects.*
- *Explain polymorphism.*

10.1 Defining Classes

A class (like structure) is a programmer-defined data type. But a class is more than a structure in that it contains both data (variables) and methods (functions). The data and functions of a class are called *class members*. Classes form the basis for object-oriented programming (OOP).

A **class** acts as a container/template. It **encapsulates** both data and functions. Once a class is defined, you can create instances of that class called **objects**. The objects then can access both its data and class members.

In general, only functions in a class are allowed to access its private data members. They are not allowed to access the private data members of another class. This provides a certain degree of security.

A class template has two parts/sections: **declaration section** and **implementation section** as shown in Figure 10.1.

Figure 10.1: A class template

```
// class declaration

class employee
{
    int id;
    double salary;
    void assign_values (const int, const double);
    void display_values();
};

// class implementation

void employee::assign_values(const int id2, const double salary2)
{
    id = id2;
    salary = salary2;
}
```

```
void employee::display_values()
{
    cout << "\nEmployee id: " << id;
    cout << "\nEmployee salary: " << salary;
}
```

The declaration section contains the keyword `class` and the class name (e.g. `employee`) followed by a pair of braces { } containing member variables (e.g., `id, salary`) and member function prototypes (e.g., `assign_values(), display_values()`). Note that there is a semicolon (;) terminating the class declaration.

The implementation section contains the function code with several parts as shown below.

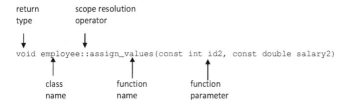

The keyword `void` tells that the function will not `return` any value to the calling function. The class name (`employee`) is followed by the scope resolution operator (`::`), the function name and its parameters. The scope resolution operator tells that function `assign_values()` belongs to the `employee` class.

The declaration of the second function is similar except that it has no parameters.

        void employee::display_values()

Here, class `employee` has data members `id` and `salary` and function members `assign_values()` and `display_values()`. The declaration part contains function the prototypes while the implementation part contains the function code. This is the general layout for class declaration.

10.2 Data Hiding

A class encapsulates both data and functions. Only the member functions are allowed to access the private data members of a class. Functions from other classes are not allowed to access its private data members.

Data hiding makes private data members of a class inaccessible to external functions from another class. This is achieved by declaring data members as `private`. For example, in the above `employee` class, variables `id` and `salary` are declared `private` so they cannot be accessed by functions outside the class.

The **access specifier** specifies the degree of access allowed for a class member (data or method). By default, all class members are `private`.

However, for classes to be useful, they must allow external functions to access their member functions.

A class declaration generally takes the form

```
class class-name
{
```

```
    private:
            // variable declaration
            // function declaration

    public:
            // variable declaration
            // function declaration
}
```

The keywords `private` and `public` specify the degree of access granted to an external function. By default, all class members are `private,` meaning, they cannot be accessed by non-member functions.

However, `public` members of a class can be accessed by member and non-member functions.

Figure 10.2 illustrates the scope of access to class members. The data and functions in the private section can only be accessed by functions in the private section. External functions cannot access its private members. However, they can still access the primate members *indirectly* by calling the `public` member functions in that class.

In general, most data members will be `private` while most function members will be `public.`

Figure 10.2: Scope of access on class members

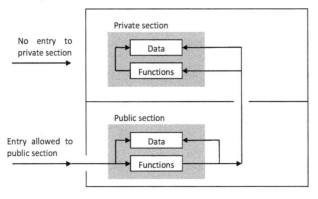

You can use the keywords `private` and `public` to specify the degree of access you want to give to a class member as shown in Figure 10.3.

Figure 10.3: Specifying access to class members

```
class employee
{
    private:
        string name;
        int mark;
    public:
        void get_input ();
        void display_info();
};

// class implementation
void student::get_input ()
{
```

```
        cout << "Enter name: ";
        cin >> name;
        cout << "Enter mark: ";
        cin >> mark;
}

void student::display_info()
{
        cout << "\nName: " << name;
        cout << "\nMark: " << mark << endl;
}
```

Here, data members name and mark are declared private while function members get_input() and display_info() are declared public. That means, variables name and mark can only be accessed by functions get_input() and display_info(). External functions cannot access these data members. However, functions get_input() and display_info() can be accessed by any function. This is because their scope is public. Program 10.1 illustrates this.

Program 10.1

```
// illustrates classes
#include "pch.h"
#include <iostream>
#include <string>
using namespace std;

// class declaration
class student
{
private:
        string name;
        int mark;
public:
        void get_input();
        void display_info();
}; // semicolon terminates class

// class methods
void student::get_input()
{
        cout << "Enter name: ";
        cin >> name;
        cout << "Enter mark: ";
        cin >> mark;
}

void student::display_info()
{
        cout << "\nName: " << name;
        cout << "\nMark: " << mark << endl;
}

// main program
void main()
{
        student stud;          // declare student object
        stud.get_input();      // get input
        stud.display_info();   // display info
}
```

Sample output

```
Enter name: Sally
Enter mark: 77
```

10.3 Scope of Variables

Variables declared inside a function have local scope, i.e., they are not visible outside the function. The scope resolution operator (: :) identifies a member function as being within the class scope.

The declaration

```
void employee::assign values(const int id2, const double salary2)
{
    id = id2;
    salary = salary2;
}
```

tells function assign_values () belonging to class employee will take in two parameters – id2 and salary2 but will not return any value to the calling function as its type is void.

10.4 Creating Objects

You can declare many instances of a class. For example, you can create three objects from the employee class as follows:

```
        employee emp1, emp2, emp3;
```

The compiler will automatically allocate memory for the data members of each of these objects.

However, for member functions, the compiler will only store one copy of each function irrespective of the number of objects created. This is because all objects share the same functions. So there is no need for separate copies of these functions for each object.

Figure 10.4 illustrates how objects are stored.

Figure 10.4: Objects in memory

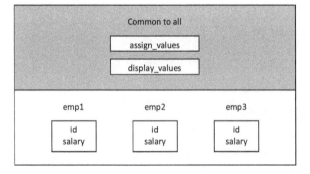

You can create arrays of objects. For example, we can declare the three employee objects more compactly as follows:

```
employee emp[3]; // array of 3 employee objects
```

The statement declares three employee objects - emp[0], emp[1] and emp[2].

You can then use a loop to access all the objects in the array. For example, you can initialize the variables id and salary to zero of every employee as follows:

```
for (i=0; i<3; i++)
{
    emp[i].id = 0;
    emp[i].salary = 0.0;
}
```

Similarly, we can display the attributes of all employees as follows:

```
for (i=0; i<3; i++)
{
    emp[i].display_values();
}
```

Program 10.2 creates an array of n=3 student objects. It reads the data using get_input() and displays the details using display_info().

Program 10.2

```
#include "pch.h"
#include <iostream>
#include <string>
#define n 3
using namespace std;

class student
{
private:
        string name;
        int mark;
public:
        void get_input();
        void display_info();
};

void student::get_input()
{
        cout << "\nEnter name: ";
        cin >> name;
        cout << "Enter mark: ";
        cin >> mark;
}

void student::display_info()
{
        cout << "\nName: " << name;
        cout << "\nMark: " << mark;
}

void main()
{
        int i;
```

```
      student stud[n];  // array of objects

      for (i = 0; i < n; i++)          // get input
            stud[i].get_input();

      for (i = 0; i < n; i++)
            stud[i].display_info(); // print output
}
```

Sample output

```
Enter name: Sally
Enter mark: 77
Enter name: Wong
Enter mark: 68
Enter name: Johnson
Enter mark: 45

Name: Sally
Mark: 77

Name: Wong
Mark: 68

Name: Johnson
Mark: 45
```

Program 10.3 (modified version of Program 10.2) illustrates the same but also computes the grades using the function get_grade().

Program 10.3

```
#include "pch.h"
#include <iostream>
#include <string>
#define n 3
using namespace std;

class student
{
private:
      string grade, name;
      int mark;
public:
      void get_input();
      void get_grade();
      void display_info();
};

void student::get_input()
{
      cout << "\nEnter name: ";
      cin >> name;
      cout << "Enter mark: ";
      cin >> mark;
}

void student::get_grade()
{
      if (mark < 50)
            grade = "Fail";
      else grade = "Pass";
}
```

```
void student::display_info()
{
      cout << "\n" << name <<"\t" << mark  << "\t" << grade;
}

// main program
void main()
{
      int i;
      student stud[n];
      for (i = 0; i < n; i++)
            stud[i].get_input();

      for (i = 0; i < n; i++)
            stud[i].get_grade();

      cout << "\nExam Results\n";
      for (i = 0; i < n; i++)
            stud[i].display_info();
}
```

Sample output

```
Enter name: Sally
Enter mark: 77

Enter name: Wong
Enter mark: 68

Enter name: Johnson
Enter mark: 48

Exam Results

Sally    77      Pass
Wong     68      Pass
Johnson  48      Fail
```

10.5 Static Class Members

When a class is instantiated, the compiler automatically allocates a block of memory for each object's data members. Thus if you create three objects, the compiler will allocate three blocks of memory.

What if a data contains a *common value* for all instances? For example, all employees in a company will have the same company name (say, co_id).

If you want a data member to store a common value for all instances, you declare it as **static**. A static member will have the *same* value for all class instances. All objects in the class will share the same memory. That variable is called a *class variable*, not an *instance variable*. Figure 10.5 illustrates this. Here, co_id is a class variable whereas id and salary are instance variables.

Figure 10.5: All three class instances share the same co_id

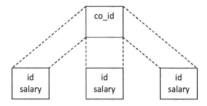

Program 10.4 illustrates static data members. It declares co_id as static and assigns the value 123. All instances share the same co_id value.

Program 10.4

```
#include "pch.h"
#include <iostream>
#include <string>
using namespace std;

class employee
{
    private:
        static int com_id; // declare com_id as static variable
        int id;
        double salary;

    public:
        void assign_values(const int, const double);
        void display_values();
};

// define static class member
int employee::com_id = 123;

void employee::assign_values(const int id2, const double salary2)
{
        id = id2;
        salary = salary2;
}

void employee::display_values()
{
        cout << "\nCompany id: " << com_id;
        cout << "\nEmployee id: " << id;
        cout << "\nEmployee salary: " << salary;
}

void main()
{
        int i, j;
        employee emp[3];   // declare 3 employee objects
        for (i = 0; i < 3; i++)
        {
                j = i + 1; // using j to assign some salary
                emp[i].assign_values(j, (float)j*500.00);
                emp[i].display_values();
                cout << endl;
        }
}
```

Output

```
Company id: 123
Employee id: 1
Employee salary: 500

Company id: 123
Employee id: 2
Employee salary: 1000

Company id: 123
Employee id: 3
Employee salary: 1500
```

10.6 The `this` Pointer

While each class instance has its own *data members*, all instances share the same *function members*. For example, for if you create several `employee` instances as shown below.

```
employee manager, supervisor, foreman;
```

All three employee objects will share the same function, e.g. `display_values()`. You can call the function as follows:

```
manager.display_values();
supervisor.display_values();
foreman.display_values();
```

C++ uses a special pointer called **this** to access the *current* member function. For example, if you call the function

```
manager.display values();
```

the compiler will use `employee *this` as follows:

```
manager.display values(employee *this);
```

The actual function call will take the form

```
display_values(&manager);
```

Similarly, if you call the function

```
foreman.display_values();
```

the actual function call will be

```
display_values(&foreman);
```

Let's explain how this further. The `assign_values()` takes in parameters `id` and `salary`. In addition, it receives a pointer to the object. Thus when you call the function

```
manager.assign_values(222, 3000.00);
```

the compiler will use the actual parameters to assign values as follows:

142

```
assign_values(employee *this, const int id, const double salary);
```

The actual function call used by the compiler is

```
assign_values(&manager, 222, 3000.00);
```

The *first* argument passed to the function (and sometimes the only argument) is a pointer to the object.

You can use the compound operator this-> to access the data members inside a function as follows:

```
void employee::display_values()
{
    cout << "\nCompany id: " << this->co_id;
    cout << "\nEmployee id: " << this->id;
    cout << "\nEmployee salary: " << this->salary;
}
```

10.7 Polymorphism

Poly means assuming different forms in different contexts. A function is said to be *polymorphic* if it has the same name but behaves differently for different objects.

Program 10.5 illustrates this. The functions assign_values() and display_values() assign and display different information for different class instances. The assign_values() has three parameters for employee and customer objects but only two parameters for supplier object. The parameters are also not all of the same type.

Program 10.5

```
#include "pch.h"
#include <iostream>
#include <string>

using namespace std;

class employee
{
private:
    int emp_id;
    double emp_salary;
public:
    void assign_values(const int id, const double salary);
    void display_values();
};

void employee::assign_values(const int id, const double salary)
{
    emp_id = id;
    emp_salary = salary;
}

void employee::display_values()
{
    cout << "\nEmployee id: " << emp_id;
    cout << "\nEmployee salary: " << emp_salary;
    cout << endl;
}
```

```cpp
class customer
{
private:
    int cus_id;
    double cus_balance;
public:
    void assign_values(const int id, const double balance);
    void display_values();
};

void customer::assign_values(const int id, const double balance)
{
    cus_id = id;
    cus_balance = balance;
}
void customer::display_values()
{
    cout << "\nCustomer id: " << cus_id;
    cout << "\nCustomer balance: " << cus_balance;
    cout << endl;
}

class supplier
{
private:
    int sup_id;
    int sup_tel;
public:
    void assign_values(const int id, const int tel);
    void display_values();
};

void supplier::assign_values(const int id, const int tel)
{
    sup_id = id;
    sup_tel = tel;
}

void supplier::display_values()
{
    cout << "\nSupplier id: " << sup_id;
    cout << "\nSupplier tel: " << sup_tel;
    cout << endl;
}

void main()
{
    employee emp; // declare employee object
    customer cus; // declare customer object
    supplier sup; // declare supplier object
    emp.assign_values(11, 555.55);
    emp.display_values();
    cus.assign_values(22, 777.77);
    cus.display_values();
    sup.assign_values(33, 12345);
    sup.display_values();
}
```

Output

```
Employee id: 11
Employee salary: 555.55
```

144

```
Customer id: 22
Customer balance: 777.77

Supplier id: 33
Supplier tel: 12345
```

10.8 Constructors

A **constructor** is a special function which has the same name as the class name. The constructor is automatically called when an object is created. No *explicit* calling is required. It is typically used for allocating memory or for initializing variables.

A constructor differs from a normal function in the following ways:

1. The constructor has the same name as the class name.

2. It does not return a value; therefore, it does not have a type specifier.

3. You can pass arguments to a constructor.

4. It is automatically called when an object is created.

Program 10.6 illustrates how a constructor works.

Program 10.6

```cpp
#include "pch.h"
#include <iostream>
#include <string>
using namespace std;

class employee
{
private:
        int id;
        double salary;

public:
        employee(); // has same name as class and no type
        void get_input();
        void display_info();
};

employee::employee() // constructor
{
        cout << "\nEntering constructor";
        id = 0;
        salary = 0.0;
        cout << "\nExiting constructor";
}

void employee::get_input()
{
        cout << "\n\nEnter id: ";
        cin >> id;
        cout << "\nEnter salary: ";
        cin >> salary;
}
```

```
void employee::display_info()
{
    cout << "\nEmployee id: " << id;
    cout << "\nEmployee salary: " << salary << endl;
}

void main()
{
    employee emp;           // create object
    emp.display_info();     // show constructor initialized values
    emp.get_input();        // get input
    emp.display_info();     // display info
}
```

Output

```
Entering constructor
Exiting constructor
Employee id: 0
Employee salary: 0


Enter id: 333

Enter salary: 5678

Employee id: 333
Employee salary: 5678
```

The constructor is called every time an object is created. That means, if there are two instances of `employee`, the constructor will be called twice as Program 10.7 illustrates.

Program 10.7

```
#include "pch.h"
#include <iostream>
#include <string>
using namespace std;

class employee
{
private:
    int id;
    double salary;

public:
    employee(); // prototype for constructor
    void get_input(const int, const double);
    void display_info();
};

// constructor for employee object
employee::employee()
{
    cout << "\nEntering constructor";
    id = 0;
    salary = 0.0;
    cout << "\nExiting constructor";
}
void employee::get_input(const int id2, const double salary2)
{
    id = id2;
```

146

```
        salary = salary2;
}

void employee::display_info()
{
        cout << "\n\nEmployee id: " << id;
        cout << "\nEmployee salary: " << salary;
}

void main()
{
        employee emp1, emp2;
        emp1.get_input(111, 500.00);
        emp1.display_info();
        emp2.get_input(222, 700.00);
        emp2.display_info();
        cout << endl;
}
```

Sample output

```
Entering constructor
Exiting constructor
Entering constructor
Exiting constructor

Employee id: 111
Employee salary: 500

Employee id: 222
Employee salary: 700
```

Overloading Constructors

Constructors can be overloaded by supplying different number of parameters and types.

Program 10.8 illustrates constructors and constructor overloading.

Program 10.8

```
#include "pch.h"
#include <iostream>
#include <string>
using namespace std;

class employee
{
private:
        int id;
        double salary;

public:
        employee();
        employee(const int id, const double salary);
        void get_input(const int, const double);
        void display_info();
};

// constructor for part-time employee
employee::employee()
{
        cout << "\nEntering constructor for part-time employee";
```
147

```
        id = 0;
        salary = 0.0;
        cout << "\nExiting constructor for part-time employee";
}

// constructor for full-time employee
employee::employee(const int id2, const double salary2)
{
        cout << "\nEntering constructor for full-time employee";
        id = id2;
        salary = 500.0 + salary2;
        cout << "\nExiting constructor for part-time employee";
}

void employee::get_input(const int id2, const double salary2)
{
        id = id2;
        salary = salary2;
}
void employee::display_info()
{
        cout << "\nEmployee id: " << id;
        cout << "\nEmployee salary: " << salary;
        cout << endl;
}

void main()
{
        employee joe; // first constructor is called
        joe.get_input(111, 500.00);
        joe.display_info();
        employee mary(555, 900.00); // second constructor is called
        mary.get_input(222, 700.00);
        mary.display_info();
}
```

Output

```
Entering constructor for part-time employee
Exiting constructor for part-time employee
Employee id: 111
Employee salary: 500

Entering constructor for full-time employee
Exiting constructor for part-time employee
Employee id: 222
Employee salary: 700
```

8.2 Destructors

A **destructor** is also a special function which has the same name as the class name but has a *tilde* (~) in front of it. It is automatically called when an object is deleted. It is typically used to reclaim memory and to perform close-up operations like displaying totals or summaries.

The following rules apply for destructors:

1. A destructor has the same name as the class name, but with a tilde (~) in front.

2. It does not return a value; therefore it has no type specifier.

3. It cannot pass any arguments (like constructors).

4. Only one destructor is allowed for each class.

5. It is called automatically when an object is deleted.

Program 10.9 illustrates destructors.

Program 10.9

```
#include "pch.h"
#include <iostream>
#include <string>
using namespace std;

class employee
{
private:
      int id;
      double salary;

public:
      employee();          // prototype for constructor
      ~employee();         // prototype for destructor
      void get_input(const int, const double);
      void display_info();
};

employee::employee()   // constructor
{
      cout << "\nEntering constructor";
      id = 0;
      salary = 0.0;
      cout << "\nExiting constructor";
}

employee::~employee() // destructor
{
      cout << "\nEntering destructor";
      cout << "\nExiting constructor";
      cout << endl;
}

void employee::get_input(const int id2, const double salary2)
{
      id = id2;
      salary = salary2;
}

void employee::display_info()
{
      cout << "\nEmployee id: " << id;
      cout << "\nEmployee salary: " << salary;
}
void main()
{
      employee emp;
      emp.display_info();   // constructor initialized values
      emp.get_input(111, 500.00);
      emp.display_info();
}
```

149

Output

```
Entering constructor
Exiting constructor
Employee id: 0
Employee salary: 0
Employee id: 111
Employee salary: 500
Entering destructor
Exiting constructor
```

10.8 Sample Programs

Program 10.10 declares an employee class with functions get_input() and display_info().

Program 10.10

```cpp
#include "pch.h"
#include <iostream>
#include <string>
using namespace std;

class employee
{
private:
    int id;
    string name;
    double salary;
public:
    void get_input(const int, const string, const double);
    void display_info();
};

void employee::get_input(const int id2, const string name2, const double salary2)
{
    id = id2;
    name = name2;
    salary = salary2;
}

void employee::display_info()
{
    cout << "\nid: \t" << id;
    cout << "\nname: \t" << name;
    cout << "\nsalary:\t" << salary;
}

void main()
{
    employee emp;
    emp.get_input(11, "Wong Mei Ling", 700.55);
    cout << "Employee information:\n";
    emp.display_info();
}
```

Output

```
Employee information:
```

```
id:      11
name:    Wong Mei Ling
salary:  700.55
```

Program 10.11 declares a student class with variables stud_id, stud_mark and stud_grade and functions get_mark(), compute_grade() and show_grade(). It uses these functions to read, compute and display student results.

Program 10.11

```cpp
#include "pch.h"
#include <iostream>
#include <string>
#define n 3
using namespace std;

class student
{
private:
     int id;
     int mark;
     char grade;
public:
     void get_mark();
     void compute_grade();
     void show_grade();
};

void student::get_mark()
{
     cout << "Enter id: ";
     cin >> id;
     cout << "Enter mark: ";
     cin >> mark;
}

void student::compute_grade()
{
     if (mark < 50)
          grade = 'F';
     else if (mark < 60)
          grade = 'C';
     else if (mark < 70)
          grade = 'B';
     else
          grade = 'A';
}

void student::show_grade()
{
     cout << id << "\t\t";
     cout << mark << "\t";
     cout << grade << endl;
}

void main()
{
     int i;
     student stud[n]; // declare 3 students
     for (i = 0; i < 3; i++)
          stud[i].get_mark();

     for (i = 0; i < 3; i++)
```

```
        stud[i].compute_grade();

    cout << "Exam Results\n\n";
    cout << "No. Name\tMark\tGrade\n";
    for (i = 0; i < 3; i++)
    {
        cout << i + 1 << "    ";
        stud[i].show_grade();
    }
}
```

Sample run

```
Enter id: 111
Enter mark: 88
Enter id: 222
Enter mark: 67
Enter id: 333
Enter mark: 45
Exam Results

No. Name      Mark    Grade
1    111       88      A
2    222       67      B
3    333       45      F
```

Program 10.12 illustrates function overloading. Functions `sum()` and `display_sum()` are both overloaded. The `sum()` takes in two parameters of type `int` in class `int_number` and three parameters of type `float` in class `float_number`. The `display_sum()` displays both integer sum and floating-point sum.

Program 10.12

```
#include "pch.h"
#include <iostream>
#include <string>
using namespace std;

class numbers
{
    int x1, x2, sumx;
    double y1, y2, y3, sumy;
    public:
    void isum(int, int);
    void dsum(double, double, double);
    void display_isum();
    void display_dsum();
};

// overloaded functions
void numbers::isum(int x1, int x2)
{
    sumx = x1 + x2;
}

void numbers::dsum(double y1, double y2, double y3)
{
    sumy = y1 + y2 + y3;
}

void numbers::display_isum()
{
    cout << "\nSum of integers = " << sumx;
```

```
}

void numbers::display_dsum()
{
        cout << "\nSum of doubles = " << sumy << endl;
}


void main()
{
        int x1 = 5, x2 = 7;
        double y1 = 10, y2 = 20, y3 = 30;
        numbers x;
        x.isum(x1, x2);
        x.display_isum();
        x.dsum(y1, y2, y3);
        x.display_dsum();
}
```

Output

```
Sum of integers = 12
Sum of doubles = 60
```

Program 10.13 illustrates static variables. It uses four instance variables act_no, balance and interest, but one class variable rate.

Program 10.13

```
#include "pch.h"
#include <iostream>
#include <string>
#define n 3
using namespace std;

class account
{
        int act_no;
        double balance;
        double interest;
        static double rate;
public:
        void get_balance();
        void compute_interest();
        void display_interest();
};

double account::rate = 0.07; // only one instance

void account::get_balance()
{
        cout << "\nAccount no: ";
        cin >> act_no;
        cout << "Account balance: ";
        cin >> balance;
}

void account::compute_interest()
{
        interest = balance * rate;
}
```

```
void account::display_interest()
{
      cout << act_no << "   ";
      cout << balance << "      ";
      cout << interest << "   ";
      cout << endl;
}


void main()
{
      int i;
      double bal = 1000.00;
      account customer[n];

      for (i = 0; i < n; i++)
      {
            customer[i].get_balance();
            customer[i].compute_interest();
      }

      cout << "\nNo. Acct   Balance    Interest\n";
      for (i = 0; i < n; i++)
      {
            cout << i + 1 << "   ";
            customer[i].display_interest();
      }

}
```

Sample run

```
Account no: 111
Account balance: 5555

Account no: 222
Account balance: 6666

Account no: 333
Account balance: 4444

No. Acct  Balance   Interest
1   111   5555      388.85
2   222   6666      466.62
3   333   4444      311.08
```

Program 10.14 is a simple example of ATM banking. It uses classes current and saving and functions open_account(), deposit(), withdraw() and show_balance().

Program 10.14

```cpp
#include "pch.h"
#include <iostream>
#include <string>
using namespace std;

class current
{
      int acct_no;
      double balance;
      public:
      void open_account();
```
154

```cpp
        void deposit();
        void withdraw();
        void show_balance();
};
void current::open_account()
{
        cout << "\nOpening current account...";
        cout << "\nEnter account number: ";
        cin >> acct_no;
        cout << "\nEnter starting amount: $";
        cin >> balance;
}

void current::deposit()
{
        int acct;
        double amount;
        cout << "\nDeposit into current account...";
        cout << "\nEnter account number: ";
        cin >> acct;
        if (acct != acct_no)
        {
                cout << "\nInvalid account - Try again";
        }
        else
        {
                cout << "\nEnter amount to deposit: $";
                cin >> amount;
                balance = balance + amount;
                cout << "\nYour new balance is $" << balance << endl;
        }
}

void current::withdraw()
{
        int acct;
        double amount;
        cout << "\nWithdrawal from current account...";
        cout << "\nEnter account number: ";
        cin >> acct;
        if (acct != acct_no)
        {
                cout << "\nInvalid account - Try again";
                return;
        }
        else
        {
                cout << "\nEnter amount to withdraw: $";
                cin >> amount;
                if (amount > balance)
                {
                        cout << "\nSorry, insufficient balance";
                }
                else
                {
                        cout << "\nPlease collect your cash";
                        balance = balance - amount;
                        cout << "\nYour new balance is $" << balance << endl;
                }
        }
}
```

```
void current::show_balance()
{
      int acct;
      cout << "\nShow current account balance";
      cout << "\nEnter account number: ";
      cin >> acct;
      if (acct == acct_no)
            cout << "\nYour balance is $" << balance;
      else
            cout << "\nInvalid account - Try again";
}

class saving
{
      int acct_no;
      double balance;
public:
      void open_account();
      void deposit();
      void withdraw();
      void show_balance();
};

void saving::open_account()
{
      cout << "\nOpen saving account...";
      cout << "\nEnter account number: ";
      cin >> acct_no;
      cout << "\nEnter starting amount: $";
      cin >> balance;
}

void saving::deposit()
{
      int acct;
      double amount;
      cout << "\nDeposit into saving account...";
      cout << "\nSaving account deposit";
      cout << "\nEnter account number: ";
      cin >> acct;
      if (acct != acct_no)
      {
            cout << "\nInvalid account - Try again";
      }
      else
      {
            cout << "\nEnter amount: $";
            cin >> amount;
            balance = balance + amount;
      }
}

void saving::withdraw()
{
      int acct;
      double amount;
      cout << "\nWithdraw from saving account...";
      cout << "\nEnter account number: ";
      cin >> acct;
      if (acct == acct_no)
      {
            cout << "\nEnter amount to withdraw: $";
            cin >> amount;
```

```
        if (amount > balance)
        {
                cout << "\nSorry, insufficient balance";
        }
        else
        {
                cout << "\nPlease collect your cash";
                balance = balance - amount;
                cout << "\nYour new balance is $" << balance;
        }
    }
}

void saving::show_balance()
{
    int acct;
    cout << "\nShowing saving account balance...";
    cout << "\nEnter account number: ";
    cin >> acct;
    if (acct == acct_no)
        cout << "\nYour balance is $" << balance;
    else
        cout << "\nInvalid account - Try again";
}

void main()
{
    current cur;
    saving sav;
    char transaction_type;
    char act_type;
    cout << "Welcome to MyBank:";

    for (; ; )  // infinite loop
    {
        while (1)  // infinite loop
        {
                cout << "\nTransaction types:";
                cout << "\nO - Open account";
                cout << "\nD - Deposit";
                cout << "\nW - Withdraw";
                cout << "\nB - Balance";
                cout << "\nX - Exit";
                cout << "\nEnter choice: ";
                cin >> transaction_type;
                transaction_type = toupper(transaction_type);
                if (transaction_type == 'X')
                    return;
                if (transaction_type == 'O' || 'D' || 'W' || 'B')
                    break;
                else
                    cout << "\nInvalid type - Try again";
        }

        while (1)
        {
                cout << "\nAccount types: ";
                cout << "\nC - Current";
                cout << "\nS - Saving";
                cout << "\nX - Exit";
                cout << "\nPlease enter account type: ";
                cin >> act_type;
                act_type = toupper(act_type);
```

```
                    if (act_type == 'X')
                         return;
                    if (act_type == 'C' || 'S')
                         break;
                    else
                         cout << "\nInvalid type - Try again";
          }

          switch (transaction_type)
          {
               case 'O':    if (act_type == 'C')
                                 cur.open_account();
                            else
                                 sav.open_account();
                            break;

               case 'D':    if (act_type == 'C')
                                 cur.deposit();
                            else
                                 sav.deposit();
                            break;

               case 'W':    if (act_type == 'C')
                                 cur.withdraw();
                            else
                                      sav.withdraw();
                            break;

               case 'B':    if (act_type == 'C')
                                 cur.show_balance();
                            else
                                 sav.show_balance();
                            break;

               case 'X':    break;

               default:     cout << "\nInvalid type - Try again";
          }
     }
}
```

Sample run

```
Welcome to MyBank:

Transaction types:
O - Open account
D - Deposit
W - Withdraw
B - Balance
X - Exit
Enter choice: O


Account types:
C - Current
S - Saving
X - Exit
Please enter account type: S

Open saving account...
Enter account number: 111
```

```
Enter starting amount: $5000

Transaction types:
O - Open account
D - Deposit
W - Withdraw
B - Balance
X - Exit
Enter choice: D

Account types:
C - Current
S - Saving
X - Exit
Please enter account type: S

Deposit into saving account...
Saving account deposit
Enter account number: 111

Enter amount: $700

Transaction types:
O - Open account
D - Deposit
W - Withdraw
B - Balance
X - Exit
Enter choice: W

Account types:
C - Current
S - Saving
X - Exit
Please enter account type: S

Withdraw from saving account...
Enter account number: 111

Enter amount to withdraw: $300

Please collect your cash
Your new balance is $5400

Transaction types:
O - Open account
D - Deposit
W - Withdraw
B - Balance
X - Exit
Enter choice: B


Account types:
C - Current
S - Saving
X - Exit
Please enter account type: S

Showing saving account balance...
Enter account number: 111

Your balance is $5400
```

```
Transaction types:
O - Open account
D - Deposit
W - Withdraw
B - Balance
X - Exit
Enter choice: X
```

Program 10.15 demonstrates how an object from one class can call another class' object. Here, the student object stud calls the message class to display a message.

Program 10.15

```cpp
#include "pch.h"
#include <iostream>
#include <string>
#define n 3
using namespace std;

class message
{
    private:
        string msg;
    public:
        void say_msg(char);
};

void message::say_msg(char result)
{
    if (result == 'P')
        cout << "Congratulations - you passed!" << endl;
    else
        cout << "Sorry - you failed!" << endl;
}

class student
{
    private:
        int id;
        int mark;
        char grade;
    public:
        void get_mark();
        void compute_grade();
        void show_result();
};

void student::get_mark()
{
    cout << "\nEnter id: ";
    cin >> id;
    cout << "Enter mark: ";
    cin >> mark;
}

void student::compute_grade()
{
    if (mark < 50)
        grade = 'F';
    else
        grade = 'P';
}
```

```
void student::show_result()
{
    message m;          // message object
    cout << "\nId: " << id;
    cout << "\nMark: " << mark;
    cout << "\nGrade: " << grade << endl;
    m.say_msg(grade); // call say_msg
}

void main()
{
    int i;
    student stud;
    for (i = 0; i < n; i++)
    {
        stud.get_mark();
        stud.compute_grade();
        stud.show_result();
    }
}
```

Sample run

```
Enter id: 111

Enter mark: 77

Id: 111
Mark: 77
Grade: P
Congratulations - you passed!

Enter id: 222

Enter mark: 44

Id: 222
Mark: 44
Grade: F
Sorry - you failed!

Enter id: 333

Enter mark: 50

Id: 333
Mark: 50
Grade: P
Congratulations - you passed!
```

Exercise

1. Write a program to implement the class `Student` with the following attributes and methods:

   Attributes
   ```
   stud_id      -   string
   stud_name    -   string
   Mark         -   integer
   ```

   Methods
   ```
   get_data()         - to get data from keyboard for stud_id, stud_name and mark
   compute_grade()    - to compute the grade (A:80-100, B:60-79, C: 50-59, F: 0-49)
   display_grade()    - to display stud_id, stud_name, mark and grade
   ```

2. Do question 1 for n=5 students. Also calculate and display the average.

3. Write a program to create and implement the class `employee`, which will have the following attributes and methods:

   Attributes

emp_id	-	string
emp_name	-	string
hours_worked	-	double
Rate	-	static double fixed 55.00

   Methods
   ```
   get_data()       - to get data from keyboard for emp_id, emp_name and
                        hours_worked
   compute_salary() - to compute salary (salary = hours_worked * rate)

   display_grade()  - to display emp_id, emp_name, hours_worked and salary
   ```

4. Do question 3 for n=7 employees. The salary is now calculated as follows: For the first 40 hours worked, the rate is as given and for the remaining hours the rate is twice that amount.

5. Distinguish between static and instance variables. Write code to show the difference between the two.

6. What is polymorphism? What purpose does it serve? Write code to illustrate polymorphism.

Chapter 9

Inheritance

Learning Outcomes:

After completing this chapter, the student will be able to

- *Explain class inheritance.*
- *Explain base (super) and derived (sub) classes.*
- *Create a class hierarchy.*
- *Override base class functions.*
- *Explain multiple class inheritance.*

11.1 What is Inheritance?

A class can inherit the data and function members of another class. The class that inherits is called **derived, sub, or child class** while the class that supplies inheritance is called **base, super, or parent class**. The base class typically contains *general* features while the derived classes contain *specific* features.

A derived class inherits data and function members of a base class. For example, we can derive current and saving classes from the base class account as shown in Figure 11.1. This is an example of *one-level inheritance*.

Figure 11.1: One-level inheritance

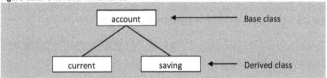

Class inheritance can take *multiple levels*. For example, from the base class person, we can derive subclasses employee and student. Then from the employee class we can derive subclasses local_employee and foreign_employee, and from the student class we can derive subclasses local_student and foreign_student as shown in Figure 11.2. This is an example of a *two-level inheritance*.

A derived class automatically inherits the base class members. That means, you don't have to re-declare them in the derived class. You can however control the degree of inheritance by using *access specifiers* private, public, protected. Private members can only be accessed from within the class they are declared. Public members can be accessed from other classes. Protected members can only be accessed from within a class hierarchy.

Figure 10.2: Two-level inheritance

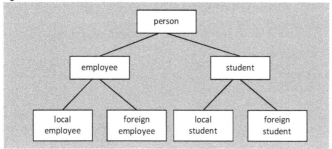

To illustrate inheritance, let's say we have the classes Person, Student and Employee with data and function members as shown in Figure 10.3.

Class	Attributes	Methods
Person	Name, Age, Sex	Add, Modify
Student	StudNo, Course	AddCourse
Employee	EmpNo, Pay	ComputePay

Figure 10.3: Inheriting data and function members

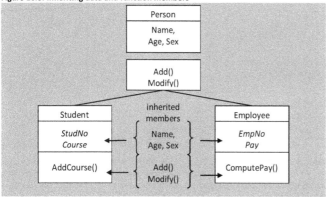

Here, Student and Employee classes are derived from Person class. Student and Employee classes inherit Name, Age and Sex attributes and functions Add() and Modify() from Person class. Student has variables StudNo and Course and function AddCourse(). Employee has variables EmpNo and Pay and function ComputePay().

11.2 Declaring Derived Classes

A derived class declaration takes the form

```
class A        // base class
{
    class A data members
    class A function members
};

class B : public A    // B is derived from A
{
    class B data members
    class B function members
}
```

Here is an example. The base class account has data members pin and name and function members open_account () and show_account (). The private access specifier tells that pin and name are private while the public access specifier tells that open_account () and show_account () are public. The private members of a class can only be accessed from within the class while public members can be accessed from within and outside the class. In general, most data members would be private and most function members would be public. Unless otherwise specified, all members are private by default.

```
// base class
class account
{
    private:
        int pin;
        string name;
    public:
        void open_account();
        void show_account();
};

// derived from the base class
class current : public account
{
    private:
        double balance;
    public:
        void deposit(const double);
        void show_deposit();
}
```

Program 11.1 illustrates class inheritance. The current class inherits from the base class account. It inherits data members acct_no and name and function members account (), open_ account () and show_acct (). In addition, current also has its own data member balance and function members deposit () and show_balance ().

Program 11.1

```
// illustrates class inheritance
#include "pch.h"
#include <iostream>
#include <string>

using namespace std;

// base class
class account
{
    protected:
            int acct_no;
```

```cpp
                string name;
    public:
            account();  // constructor
            void open_account(const int, const string);
            void show_account();
};

// derived class
class current : public account
{
        private:
            double balance;
        public:
            current();
            void deposit(const double);
            void show_balance();
};

// base class constructor
account::account()
{
    acct_no = 0;
    name = " ";
}

void account::open_account(const int acct_no2, const string name2)
{
    acct_no = acct_no2;
    name = name2;
}

void account::show_account()
{
    cout << "\n\nFrom account class...";
    cout << "\nAccount number: " << acct_no;
    cout << "\nName: " << name << endl;
}

// current class constructor
current::current()
{
    balance = 0.00;
}

void current::deposit(const double dep)
{
    balance = balance + dep;
    cout << "\nYou deposited: $" << dep;
}

void current::show_balance()
{
    cout << "\n\nFrom current class";
    cout << "\nCurrent account no: " << acct_no;
    cout << "\nName: " << name;
    cout << "\nYour balance is: ¢" << balance;
    cout << endl;
}

void main()
{
    current cur;
    cur.open_account(111, "Sally");    // from base class
```

166

```
        cur.show_account();                    // from base class
        cur.deposit(1000.00);                 // from current class
        cur.show_balance();                    // from current class
        cur.deposit(500.00);
        cur.show_balance();
}
```

Sample output:

```
From account class...
Account number: 111
Name: Sally

You deposited: $1000

From current class
Current account no: 111
Name: Sally
Your balance is: $1000

You deposited: $500

From current class
Current account no: 111
Name: Sally
Your balance is: $1500
```

Program 11.2 is an extended version of Program 11.1. It contains an additional `saving` class.

Program 11.2

```
#include "pch.h"
#include <iostream>
#include <string>
using namespace std;

class account
{
    protected:
            int acct_no;
            string name;
    public:
            account();
            void open_account(const int, const string);
            void show_account();
};
class current : public account
{
    private:
            double balance;
    public:
            current();
            void deposit(const double);
            void show_balance();
};

class saving : public account
{
    private:
            double balance;
    public:
            saving();
            void deposit(const double);
```

167

```
        void show_balance();
};

account::account()
{
      acct_no = 0;
      name = " ";
}

void account::open_account(const int acct_no2, const string name2)
{
      acct_no = acct_no2;
      name = name2;
}

void account::show_account()
{
      cout << "\n\nFrom account class...";
      cout << "\nAccount number: " << acct_no;
      cout << "\nName: " << name;
}

current::current()
{
      balance = 0.00;
}

void current::deposit(const double dep)
{
      balance = balance + dep;
      cout << "\nYou deposited: $" << dep;
}

void current::show_balance()
{
      cout << "\n\nFrom current class";
      cout << "\nAccount no: " << acct_no;
      cout << "\nYour balance is $" << balance;
}

saving::saving()
{
      balance = 0.00;
}

void saving::deposit(const double dep)
{
      balance = balance + dep;
      cout << "\nYou deposited: $" << dep;
}

void saving::show_balance()
{
      cout << "\n\nFrom saving class";
      cout << "\nAccount no: " << acct_no;
      cout << "\nYour balance is: $" << balance;
}

void main()
{
      current cur;
      saving sav;
      cur.open_account(111, "Sally");
```

168

```
        cur.show_account();
        cur.deposit(1000.00);
        cur.show_balance();
        sav.open_account(222, "Johnson");
        sav.show_account();
        sav.deposit(2000.00);
        sav.show_balance();
        cout << endl;
}
```

Sample output

```
From account class...
Account number: 111
Name: Sally
You deposited: $1000

From current class
Account no: 111
Your balance is $1000

From account class...
Account number: 222
Name: Johnson
You deposited: $2000

From saving class
Account no: 222
Your balance is: $2000
```

11.3 Overriding Base Class Functions

A derived class inherits (non-private) the base class member functions. It can also declare its own member functions with the *same* name as those in the base class but which override base class functions.

Program 11.3 illustrates overriding base class functions. It has base class person and derived class student, each with functions get_data() and display_data(). The function names are the same in both classes, but they will display different results.

Program 11.3

```cpp
#include "pch.h"
#include <iostream>
#include <string>
using namespace std;

class person
{
    protected:
        int person_id;
        string name;
    public:
        void get_input(const int, const string);
        void display_info();
};

class student : public person
{
    private:
        int stud_id, mark;
```

```
        public:
                void get_input(int, int);
                void display_info();
};

void person::get_input(const int id2, const string name2)
{
        person_id = id2;
        name = name2;
}

void person::display_info()
{
        cout << "\nPerson id: " << person_id;
        cout << "\nName: " << name;
        cout << endl;
}

void student::get_input(int stud_id2, int mark2)
{
        stud_id = stud_id2;
        mark = mark2;
}

void student::display_info()
{
        cout << "\nStudent id: " << stud_id;
        cout << "\nMark: " << mark;
        cout << endl;
}

void main()
{
        person psn;
        psn.get_input(11, "Robin");
        psn.display_info();
        student stud;
        stud.get_input(22, 77);
        stud.display_info();
        cout << endl;
}
```

Sample run

```
Person id: 11
Name: Robin

Student id: 22
Mark: 77
```

11.4 Initializing Constructors

We have already seen how constructors work. But how do they work in a class hierarchy?

Instantiating a derived class will automatically invoke base class constructor followed by the derived class constructor. That means, two constructors will be called when creating a derived class object.

Program 11.4 illustrates this.

Program 11.4

```cpp
#include "pch.h"
#include <iostream>
#include <string>
using namespace std;
class account
{
        protected:
                int acct_no;
                string name;
        public:
                void get_input();
                account()           // without using a prototype declaration
                {
                        cout << "\nFrom account class";
                }
};

class current : public account
{
        protected:
                double balance;
        public:
                current()
                {
                        cout << "\nFrom current class";
                }
                void get_deposit();
                void show_balance();
};

void account::get_input()
{
        cout << "\n\nEnter account number: ";
        cin >> acct_no;
        cout << "\nEnter name: ";
        cin >> name;
}

void current::get_deposit()
{
        cout << "\nEnter balance: ";
        cin >> balance;
}

void current::show_balance()
{
        cout << "\nYour balance is: $" << balance;
}

void main()
{
        account act;
        current cur;
        act.get_input();
        cur.get_deposit();
        cur.show_balance();
        cout << endl;
}
```

Sample output

```
From account class
From account class
From current class

Enter account number: 111

Enter name: Robin

Enter balance: 5700

Your balance is: $5700
```

11.5 Multiple Inheritance

C++ also allows a class to inherit from more than one base class. This is called **multiple inheritance**. Figure 9.4 illustrates this. The RoundTable class inherits from the base classes Table and Circle.

Figure 9.4: Creating RoundTable through two base classes

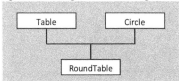

Program 11.5 illustrates multiple inheritance. It declares the class RoundTable which inherits from Table and Circle classes. The main() function calls the three functions RoundTable::Height(). RoundTable::Area() and RoundTable::Color().

Program 11.5

```cpp
// illustrates multiple inheritance
#include "pch.h"
#include <iostream>
#include <string>
using namespace std;

class Circle
{
    double radius;
    public:
        Circle(double r)
        {
            radius = r;
        }

        double Area()
        {
            return radius * radius * 3.14;
        }
};

class Table
{
    double height;
    public:
        Table(double h)
```

172

```
                {
                        height = h;
                }

                double Height()
                {
                        return height;
                }
};

// multiple inheritance
class RoundTable : public Table, public Circle
{
        string color;

public:
        RoundTable(double h, double r, string c);
        string Color()
        {
                return color;
        }
};

RoundTable::RoundTable(double h, double r, string c):Circle(r), Table(h)
{
        color = c;
}

void main()
{
        RoundTable table(15.0, 3.0, "brown");
        cout << "Your table measurements are: ";
        cout << "\nHeight = " << table.Height();
        cout << "\nArea = " << table.Area();
        cout << "\nColor = " << table.Color();
        cout << endl;
}
```

Output:

```
Your table measurements are:
Height = 15
Area = 28.26
Color = brown
```

11.6 Virtual Functions

A derived class automatically inherits its base class members. If you do not want a derived class to inherit a base class function, you can declare it as virtual. This will stop the inheritance. For example, you can stop the inheritance of the base class function display() by declaring it virtual.

Program 11.6 illustrates this. Both One and Two classes have function display(). When the show() function is called, it will call the correct function.

Program 11.6

```
// Program that illustrates virtual function
#include "pch.h"
#include <iostream>
#include <string>
```

173

```
using namespace std;

class One
{
   public:
       virtual void display()
       {
              cout << "\nClass One";
       }
};

class Two : public One
{
   public:
       virtual void display()   // overrides One's display
       {
              cout << "\nClass Two";
       }
};

void show(One ptr)   // uses pointer
{
       ptr.display();
}

void main()
{
       One one;
       Two two;
       one.display();
       two.display();
       show(one);
       show(two);
       cout << endl;
}
```

Output:
```
Class One
Class Two
Class One
Class One
```

Exercise

1. Create base class Person with data members id and name and a member function to display these values. Create a subclass Employee with data members job_title and salary, and a function to assign and display these values. Write a main() to create objects from these classes and to call the functions.

2. Create class Account with data members acct_no and balance and member functions. Derive two classes from Account – Saving with interest rate and Current with service charge. Write a program to implement these classes.

3. Create base class Book with data members ISBN, title and author. Derive two classes – Fiction containing an integer for reading level and NonFiction containing a variable for storing number of pages. Write a program to implement these classes.

Chapter 12

Friends

Learning Outcomes:

After completing this chapter, the student will be able to

- *Explain the friend feature.*
- *Declare function as a friend.*
- *Declare class as a friend.*
- *Declare a non-member function as a friend.*

12.1 The `friend` Feature

One of the strengths of **o**bject-**o**riented **p**rogramming (OOP) is *data or information hiding*. Information hiding means hiding implementation details so they are inaccessible to the private members of other classes. This provides some degree of security against unauthorized access.

However, there may be situations where a function (method) from one class may need to access the private data members of another class. To illustrate, let's suppose we have current and saving classes as shown in the code below. We want to be able to transfer funds from saving account to current account if the latter has insufficient funds.

```
class current
{
    int account_no;
    double balance;

    public:
        void open_account();
        void deposit();
        void withdraw();
        void show_balance();
};

class saving
{
    int account_no;
    double balance;

    public:
        void open_account();
        void deposit();
        void withdraw();
        void show_balance();
};
```

How can we do this?

12.2 Declaring Function as a Friend

We can do this by declaring function transfer() in current as a friend in the saving class as shown in the code below.

```
class current
{
    int account_no;
    double balance;

    public:
        void open_account();
        void deposit();
        void withdraw(); void show_balance();
        void transfer(saving &)
};

class saving
{
    int account_no;
    double balance;
    public:
        void open_account();
        void deposit();
        void withdraw();
        void show_balance();

        // declare transfer in current as friend
        friend void current::transfer(saving &)
};
```

Note the statement in the **saving** class

```
        friend void current::transfer(saving &);
```

and the statement in the **current** class

```
        void transfer(saving &);
```

Here, the parameter is passed *by reference (&)*.

Program 12.1 illustrates how the friend feature works. It allows transfer() function in current to access the private data members of saving.

Program 12.1

```
// illustrates friends
#include "pch.h"
#include <iostream>
#include <string>
using namespace std;

class saving;      // forward declaration

class current
{
    int account_no;
    double balance;

    public:
```

176

```
                void open_account();
                void deposit();
                void withdraw();
                void show_balance();
                void transfer_fund(saving &); // function prototype
};

class saving
{
      int account_no;
      double balance;


      public:
                void open_account();
                void deposit();
                void withdraw();
                void show_balance();

      // declare transfer_fund in current as friend
      friend void current::transfer_fund(saving &);
};

void current::open_account()
{
      cout << "\nOpening current account...";
      cout << "\nEnter account number: ";
      cin >> account_no;
      cout << "\nEnter starting amount: $";
      cin >> balance;
}

void current::deposit()
{
      int acct_no;
      double amount;
      cout << "\nDepositing into current account...";
      cout << "\nEnter account number: ";
      cin >> acct_no;
      if (acct_no != account_no)
      {
            cout << "\nInvalid account - try again";
      }
      else
      {
            cout << "\nEnter amount to deposit: $";
            cin >> amount;
            balance = balance + amount;
            cout << "\nYour new balance is $" << balance;
      }
}

void current::withdraw()
{
      int acct_no;
      double amount;
      cout << "\nWithdrawing from current account...";
      cout << "\nEnter your account number: ";
      cin >> acct_no;
      if (acct_no != account_no)
      {
            cout << "\nInvalid account - try again";
      }
```

```
      else
      {
            cout << "\nEnter amount to withdraw: $";
            cin >> amount;
            if (amount > balance)
            {
                  cout << "\nSorry, insufficient balance!";
            }
            else
            {
                  cout << "\nCollect your cash";
                  balance = balance - amount;
                  cout << "\nYour new balance is $" << balance;
            }
      }
}

void current::show_balance()
{
      int acct_no;
      cout << "\nCurrent account balance:";
      cout << "\nEnter account number: ";
      cin >> acct_no;
      if (acct_no == account_no)
            cout << "\nYour balance is $" << balance;
      else
            cout << "\nInvalid account - try again!";
}

// uses reference parameter
void current::transfer_fund(saving &savptr)
{
      int acct_no;
      double amount;
      cout << "\nTransfering from saving to current account...";
      cout << "\nEnter current account number: ";
      cin >> acct_no;
      if (acct_no != account_no)
      {
            cout << "\nInvalid account - try again!";
            return;
      }
      cout << "\nEnter saving account number: ";
      cin >> acct_no;
      if (acct_no != savptr.account_no)
      {
            cout << "\nInvalid account - try again";
            return;
      }
      cout << "\nEnter amount to transfer: $";
      cin >> amount;
      if (amount > savptr.balance) // saving account balance
      {
            cout << "\nInsufficient funds";
            return;
      }
      else
      {
            savptr.balance = savptr.balance - amount; // subtract
            balance = balance + amount; // add to current balance
            cout << "\nNew current balance is $" << balance;
            cout << "\nNew saving balance is $" << savptr.balance;
            cout << endl;
```

```cpp
        }
}

void saving::open_account()
{
        cout << "\nOpening saving account...";
        cout << "\nEnter account number: ";
        cin >> account_no;
        cout << "\nEnter starting amount: $";
        cin >> balance;
}

void saving::deposit()
{
        int acct_no;
        double amount;
        cout << "\nDeposit into saving account...";
        cout << "\nSaving account deposit";
        cout << "\nEnter account number: ";
        cin >> acct_no;
        if (acct_no != account_no)
        {
                cout << "\nInvalid account - try again!";
                return;
        }
        else
        {
                cout << "\nEnter amount: $";
                cin >> amount;
                balance = balance + amount;
        }
}

void saving::withdraw()
{
        int acct_no;
        double amount;
        cout << "\nWithdrawing from saving account...";
        cout << "\nEnter account number: ";
        cin >> acct_no;

        if (acct_no == account_no)
        {
                cout << "\nEnter amount to withdraw: $";
                cin >> amount;
                if (amount > balance)
                {
                        cout << "\nSorry, insufficient balance!";
                        return;
                }
                else
                {
                        cout << "\nCollect your cash";
                        balance = balance - amount;
                        cout << "\nYour new balance is $" << balance;
                }
        }
}

void saving::show_balance()
{
        int acct_no;
        cout << "\nSaving account balance:";
```

179

```
        cout << "\nEnter account number: ";
        cin >> acct_no;
        if (acct_no == account_no)
            cout << "\nYour balance is $" << balance;
        else
            cout << "\nInvalid account. Please try again";
}

void main()
{
    current cur;
    saving sav;
    char transaction_type, act_type;
    cout << "\nWelcome to MyBank:";
    for (; ;)   //infinite loop
    {
        while (1) // infinite loop
        {
            cout << "\nTransactions available:\n";
            cout << "O - Open account\n";
            cout << "D - Deposit\n";
            cout << "W - Withdraw\n";
            cout << "B - Balance\n";
            cout << "T - Transfer from saving to current\n";
            cout << "X - Exit\n";
            cout << "Enter choice: ";
            cin >> transaction_type;
            transaction_type = toupper(transaction_type);
            if (transaction_type == 'X')
                return;
            if (transaction_type == 'O' || 'D' || 'W' || 'B' || 'T')
                break;
            else
                cout << "\nInvalid type. Please try again";
        }

        if (transaction_type == 'T')
        {
            cur.transfer_fund(sav);
            return;
        }

        while (1)  // infinite loop
        {
            cout << "\n\nAccount types available";
            cout << "\nC - Current";
            cout << "\nS - Saving";
            cout << "\nX - Exit";
            cout << "\n\nEnter account type: ";
            cin >> act_type;
            act_type = toupper(act_type);
            if (act_type == 'X')
                return;
            if (act_type == 'C' || 'S')
                break;
            else
                cout << "\nInvalid type. Please try again";
        }

        switch (transaction_type)
        {
        case 'O':
            if (act_type == 'C') cur.open_account();
```

```
                else sav.open_account();
                break;
        case 'D':
                if (act_type == 'C') cur.deposit();
                else sav.deposit();
                break;
        case 'W':
                if (act_type == 'C') cur.withdraw();
                else sav.withdraw();
                break;
        case 'B':
                if (act_type == 'C') cur.show_balance();
                else sav.show_balance();
                break;
        case 'T':
                if (act_type == 'S') cur.show_balance();
                else sav.show_balance();
                break;
        case 'X': break;
        default: cout << "\nInvalid type - try again!";
        }
        cout << endl;
    }
}
```

Sample run

```
Welcome to MyBank:

Transaction available:
O - Open account
D - Deposit
W - Withdraw
B - Balance
T - Transfer fund from saving to current
E - Exit
Enter choice: O

Account types available
C - Current
S - Saving
E - Exit
Enter account type: C

Open current account...
Enter account number: 1

Enter starting amount: $100

Transaction types available
O - Open account
D - Deposit
W - Withdraw
B - Balance
T - Transfer fund from saving to current
X - Exit
Enter choice: O


Account types available
C - Current
S - Saving
X - Exit
```

```
Enter account type: S
Open saving account...
Enter account number: 2

Enter starting amount: $200

Transaction types available
O - Open account
D - Deposit
W - Withdraw
B - Balance
T - Transfer fund from saving to current
X - Exit
Enter choice: T

Transfer fund from saving to current account...
Enter current account number: 1
Enter saving account number: 2
Enter amount to transfer: $30
New current balance is $130
New saving balance is $170
```

The above code associates friend with the transfer() function in current. However, a friend function need not belong to any class, in which case the class name and the scope resolution operator (::) can be dropped and shown below.

```
friend void transfer(saving &);
```

A class may have more than one friend. In this case, the function prototypes of all friends must be declared (along with other function prototypes) in the class declaration. The keyword friend must be prefixed to the function.

When a function from one class tries to access another class' private data members, the compiler checks the function prototypes, and one of the following happens:

- The function is a member and access is granted.
- The function is a friend and access is granted.
- The function is not a member/friend and access is denied.

12.3 Declaring Class as a Friend

We can also make an entire class as friend of another class in which case all functions can access the private data members of the associated friend class. In the code below, the functions open_account(), deposit(), withdraw(), and show_balance() in current can access all the private data members of saving.

```
class current
{
    int account_no;
    double balance;

    public:
        void open_account();
        void deposit();
        void withdraw();
        void show_balance();
        void transfer(saving &);
```

```
};

class saving
{
    int account_no;
    double balance;

    public:
        void open_account();
        void deposit();
        void withdraw();
        void show balance();

        // declaring current class as friend
        friend class current;
};
```

Class friendship can be *mutual*. That is, they can be friends of each other. In this case, each class must *explicitly* declare that it is a friend of the other class. For example, if you want both current and saving to access the private data members of each other, you must declare current as a friend in saving, and saving as a friend in current as shown in the code below.

```
class current
{
    int account_no;
    double balance;

    public:
        void open_account();
        void deposit();
        void withdraw();
        void show_balance();
        void transfer(saving &);

    // declaring saving as a friend
    friend class saving;
};

class saving
{
    int account_no;
    double balance;

    public:
        void open_account();
        void deposit();
        void withdraw();
        void show_balance();
        void transfer(current &);

    // declaring current class as friend
    friend class current;
};
```

12.4 Declaring Non-class Function as a Friend

A class may declare a *non-member* function as a friend. The same non-member function can also be a friend of several classes.

Program 12.2 illustrates this. The non-member function get_total_bal() is declared as a friend in both current and saving classes. This allows get_total_bal() to access the private data members of both current and saving.

Program 12.2

```cpp
#include "pch.h"
#include <iostream>
#include <string>

using namespace std;

class saving; // forward declaration of saving class

class current
{
        int act_no;
        double balance;

public:
        void deposit();
        // prototype for friend function
        friend void get_total_bal(const current curptr, const saving savptr);
};

class saving
{
        int act_no;
        double balance;

public:
        void deposit();

        // prototype for friend function
        friend void get_total_bal(const current curptr, const saving savptr);
};

void current::deposit()
{
        cout << "\nDeposit into current account...";
        cout << "\nAccount no = ";
        cin >> act_no;
        cout << "\nAmount = ";
        cin >> balance;
        cout << "\nYour new current balance is $" << balance;
        cout << endl;
}

void saving::deposit()
{
        cout << "\nDeposit into saving account...";
        cout << "\nAccount no = ";
        cin >> act_no;
        cout << "\nAmount = ";
        cin >> balance;
        cout << "\nYour new saving balance is $" << balance;
        cout << endl;
}

// A friend function of current and saving classes
void get_total_bal(const current curptr, const saving savptr)
{
        cout << "\nTotal balance is $";
```

184

```
        cout << curptr.balance + savptr.balance;
        cout << endl;
}

void main()
{
        saving sav;
        current cur;
        cur.deposit();
        sav.deposit();
        get_total_bal(cur, sav); // call function
}
```

Sample run

```
Deposit into current account...
Account no = 1

Amount = 100

Your new current balance is $100

Deposit into saving account...
Account no = 2

Amount = 200

Your new saving balance is $200

Total balance is $300
```

Exercise

1. Create two classes: `Apartment` with attributes `apt_num` and rent, and `Tenant` with attributes name, `tel` and `apt_num`. Write a member function for `Tenant` to access and display the tenant's name and rent.

2. Create two classes: `Course` with attributes ccode and cname, and `Student` with attributes sname, ccode and mark. Write a member function for `Student` that will display the student's name, course code, course name and the grade Pass if mark is greater than or equal to 50 or the grade Fail if mark is less than 50.

3. For Question 2, write a non-member function that will display sname, ccode, cname and the grade Pass if mark is greater than or equal to 50 or the grade Fail if mark is less than 50.

4. Create classes `Current` and `Saving` each with variables acct_no and balance, and functions, deposit() and withdraw(). Write a program that allows a customer to deposit money into or withdraw money from each account. The withdraw() function should be such that if one account has insufficient fund, it should be able to access from the other account and the balances updated accordingly.

5. Do Question 4 for n = 5 customers.

References

1. N. M. Josuttis, The C++ Standard Library: A Tutorial and Reference.

2. Arthur O'Dwyer, Mastering the C++

3. Marc Gregoire, Professional C++.

4. Stanley B. Lippman, C++ Primer.

5. Bjarne Stroustrup, The C++ Programming Language.

6. http://www.cplusplus.com/doc/tutorial/

7. https://www.programiz.com/cpp-programming

8. https://www.tutorialspoint.com/cplusplus

9. https://docs.microsoft.com/en-us/cpp/visual-cpp-in-visual-studio

10. https://en.cppreference.com/w/cpp/language

11. Peter Gottschling, Discovering Modern C++: An Intensive Course for Scientists, Engineers, and Programmers.

12. Bjarne Stroustroup, Programming: Principles and Practice Using C++.

13. Ulla Kirch-Prinz, A Complete Guide to Programming in C++.

14. Todd W. Breedlove, C++: An Active Learning Approach.

YOUR KNOWLEDGE HAS VALUE